IRELAND

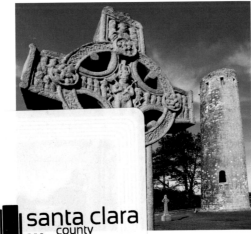

⊙ Walking Eye App

YOUR FREE EBOOK AVAILABLE THROUGH THE WALKING EYE APP

Your guide now includes a free eBook to your chosen destination, for the same great price as before. Simply download the Walking Eye App from the App Store or Google Play to access your free eBook.

HOW THE WALKING EYE APP WORKS

Through the Walking Eye App, you can purchase a range of eBooks and destination content. However, when you buy this book, you can download the corresponding eBook for free. Just see below in the grey panel where to find your free content and then scan the QR code at the bottom of this page.

Destinations: Download essential destination content featuring recommended sights and attractions, restaurants, hotels and an A–Z of practical information, all available for purchase.

Ships: Interested in ship reviews? Find independent reviews of river and ocean ships in this section, all available for purchase.

eBooks: You can download your free accompanying digital version of this guide here. You will also find a whole range of other eBooks, all available for purchase.

Free access to travel-related blog articles about different destinations, updated on a daily basis.

HOW THE EBOOKS WORK

The eBooks are provided in EPUB file format. Please note that you will need an eBook reader installed on your device to open the file. Many devices come with this as standard, but you may still need to install one manually from Google Play.

The eBook content is identical to the content in the printed guide.

HOW TO DOWNLOAD THE WALKING EYE APP

1. Download the Walking Eye App from the App Store or Google Play.
2. Open the app and select the scanning function from the main menu.
3. Scan the QR code on this page – you will then be asked a security question to verify ownership of the book.
4. Once this has been verified, you will see your eBook in the purchased ebook section, where you will be able to download it.

Other destination apps and eBooks are available for purchase separately or are free with the purchase of the Insight Guide book.

CONTENTS

Introduction

Directory

Credits

Best Routes

CELTIC ROMANCE

Glimpse the round tower through the Celtic mist at Glendalough (route 3), enjoy a kingly view from the Rock of Cashel (route 5), climb mystical Knocknarea (route 15) or venture over the sea to Skellig Michael (route 8).

RECOMMENDED ROUTES FOR...

CHILDREN

Visit a 19th-century 'coffin ship' in New Ross (route 4), get up close to the animals at Fota Wildlife Park (route 6) or play games on endless stretches of sand in County Donegal (route 15).

GARDENERS

Powerscourt Gardens (route 3) are considered among the finest in Europe. Bantry House (route 7) has terraced gardens overlooking the bay, and do not miss the Palm House in Belfast's Botanic Gardens (route 16).

LITERARY TYPES

The Book of Kells is at Trinity College (route 1), alma mater of many Irish writers, but not W.B. Yeats, who preferred Sligo (route 15). The Dublin Writers Museum (route 2) will explain why.

NATURAL WONDERS

The 40,000 basalt columns of the Giant's Causeway (route 16), the Cliffs of Moher (route 11), the view from Croagh Patrick (route 14) and the waves below Slieve League (route 15) will take your breath away.

PICTURE-BOOK VILLAGES

Choose from the pretty thatched cottages of Adare (route 10), Kinvara's stone quays and views of Galway Bay (route 11), or Lismore (route 5) with its fairy-tale castle above the wooded Blackwater Valley.

SHOPPERS

Treat yourself to some Jerpoint Glass in Kilkenny (route 4) or handwoven linens in Avoca (route 3), invest in Waterford Crystal (route 5), or go mad on the high streets in Dublin and Belfast (routes 1, 2 and 16).

WALKERS

Walk across heathery hills on the Dingle Peninsula (route 9), explore the eerie limestone plateau of the Burren (route 11) or marvel at Connemara's huge skies (route 13).

INTRODUCTION

An introduction to Ireland's geography, customs and culture, plus illuminating background information on cuisine, history and what to do when you're there.

EXPLORE IRELAND

Ireland is Europe's most westerly outpost, swathed with vast areas of unspoilt wilderness, dotted with romantic ruins and yet also boasting two of Europe's liveliest capital cities, Dublin and Belfast.

Ireland is a land of contrasts and contradictions. It is famous for having some world-class cities, yet is also a place apart as the westernmost land mass in Europe, where serried ranges of scantly inhabited hills lead to a rugged Atlantic coast, and the legacy of its Celtic and Gaelic past persists. Throughout your travels, you will encounter the contrast of the old and traditional alongside the new. Many heritage sites have bold modern architectural additions, and the 'jarveys' driving the horse-drawn sidecars in Killarney take their bookings by mobile phone.

GEOGRAPHY AND LAYOUT

The island of Ireland contains two separate countries: the Republic of Ireland and Northern Ireland. The latter, in the northeastern corner of the island, is part of the UK. In its entirety, the island covers 84,288 sq km (32,544 sq miles), measuring 485km (302 miles) at its longest point and 304km (189 miles) at its widest, while its coastline extends for around 5,630km (3,500 miles). Low ranges of mountains surround a central lowland area of limestone, much of which is covered in peat bogs.

Getting around

Public transport is a weak point. While the railways link the peripheral towns to Dublin, the lines do not interconnect to any useful extent. Neither is bus travel satisfactory for touring. If you are intending to visit rural Ireland, the only comfortable option is by car.

The routes in this guide begin with two walks exploring the historic and modern faces of the Republic of Ireland's capital, Dublin. Following these are a series of drives and walks that have been arranged to run clockwise around the country, down the east coast, along the south and up the west, ending in Northern Ireland. Wicklow, the garden of Ireland, is an easy day trip from Dublin; then the routes visit Kilkenny, Waterford and the iconic Rock of Cashel, all of which are only a short distance from the main Dublin–Cork road. After a walk through Cork's medieval streets and Victorian harbour, the routes continue along the scenic coast of west Cork and Kerry to the Dingle Peninsula, before exploring 'castle country' around the Shannon Estuary, visiting Adare, Limerick and Bunratty. The routes then proceed northwards up the more exposed

Beach on Melmore Head, County Donegal

west coast from the strange limestone plateau known as the Burren in County Clare to vibrant Galway city. A day-long drive through ruggedly beautiful Connemara leads towards charming Westport town and scenic County Mayo. Further north, Sligo town and the surrounding countryside were made famous in the poems of W.B. Yeats, while County Donegal has some lovely beaches. From here, we cross the border to visit Northern Ireland's fast-changing capital, Belfast, with a detour to the Giant's Causeway.

HISTORY AND ARCHITECTURE

The early settlers left their marks all over the land, from megalithic tombs in the Boyne Valley to the mysterious stone circles of west Cork and Kerry. Later, the flourishing of Irish monasticism in the 6th to 9th centuries bequeathed the beautiful ruins at Glendalough and Cashel. The first hostile invaders were the Vikings in the 9th century, but they, like the Anglo-Normans who followed, intermarried and were absorbed into Irish society. The rich lived in tower houses or castles, like Blarney and Bunratty, fortified against tribal warfare. They also introduced Continental orders like the Cistercians, and endowed monasteries such as Jerpoint Abbey in County Kilkenny.

Henry VIII's decision in 1541 to impose English rule – and what would become the Protestant religion – on Ireland, which shared its Catholic loyalties with England's enemies, France and Spain, had long-running repercussions. Walled towns such as Cork, Galway, Kilkenny and Waterford were used for refuge by English settlers, sent to Ireland to swell the numbers loyal to the king.

The coming of more peaceful times in the 18th and 19th centuries saw the construction of Georgian Dublin, as well as the elaborate 'big houses' (as the Irish call stately homes) scattered throughout the countryside, many with ambitious gardens.

From famine to feast

Ireland was devastated by the Great Famine of 1845–9, when about 1 million people died and another million emigrated, leaving vast tracts of land uninhabited. There followed a century of political unrest and economic depression, and only in the past few decades has Ireland recovered, changing from a backward-looking society to one of the most cosmopolitan and culturally successful (from Seamus Heaney to U2 to *Riverdance*) in Europe. The development of its tourist industry was aided by the availability of inexpensive flights, and 2013 saw a massive influx of US visitors, drawn by the Gathering celebration of Irish heritage. Irish tourism received another boost in 2016 with the release of *Star Wars Episode VII*, which featured Skellig Michael, a rugged island off Ireland's southwest coast.

Bar in Limerick

CLIMATE

Ireland has a mild maritime climate with temperate summers. July is the warmest month with temperatures averaging 14–15°C (57–9°F), and February is the coldest with averages of 4–5°C (39–41°F).

Rainfall increases as you travel west. Between December and March, cold and rainy weather can persist everywhere. In winter the days are short, with the sun setting at around 4.30pm by the solstice (21 December). In contrast, summer evenings are long, with daylight until 10pm or later. July and August are the best months for hot, sunny weather, but this is never predictable. These months are also the high season for Irish family holidays, and prices and pressure on facilities rise accordingly. The best times to visit are late spring and early autumn; May to June, and September and October.

POPULATION

The population of the Republic of Ireland is just over 4.5 million, while Northern Ireland's population is just over 1.8 million.

About 1.5 million of the Republic's population live in Dublin, which is much like any other city – fast-paced and stressful, with grid-locked traffic. Over 40 percent of the population of the Republic live within 100km (62 miles) of the city. Outside Dublin, the average density is 57 people per sq km (148 per square mile). In remote regions like west Cork and Kerry, the average falls to around 27 people per sq km. To get a feel for Ireland, it really is necessary to travel beyond Dublin.

Ireland's population declined during the 20th century, chiefly due to emigration, and only stabilised in the late-1980s, growing steadily throughout the 1990s. The expansion of the EU in 2004 led to a new wave of immigrants, chiefly from Eastern Europe, but also from Africa and Brazil, where Irish missionaries have long been active in education. While the economic downturn following the financial crisis of 2008 led to a rise in emigration – with many Eastern European workers returning home and Irish people moving overseas to find work – the Irish economy

National Library of Ireland, Dublin

Georgian doorway, Dublin   *St Mary's Church, Glendalough*

began to pick up in 2014, and population figures have begun to stabilise once more.

POLITICS AND ECONOMICS

The Republic's two main parties, both conservative, have their origins in Ireland's Civil War (1922–3): Fianna Fáil (*Warriors of Ireland*) traditionally draws its support from small farmers, the urban working class and the self-employed, while Fine Gael (*Tribe of the Irish*) is supported by big farmers and the professional classes. Left and right wing mean very little in Irish politics. Due to proportional representation, governments tend to be coalitions.

In old Gaelic society people owed allegiance to the tribal chief or *taoiseach* (pronounced 'tee-shock'). It is often suggested that Irish politics has developed along similar lines. There are many family political dynasties, with seats being handed down from father to son or daughter. One exception was Bertie Ahern, *taoiseach* (prime minister) from 1997–2008; his daughter Cecelia is a best-selling author, while daughter Georgina married Nicky Byrne of boy band Westlife.

The Troubles

From 1969, the international view of Irish politics was dominated for 30 years by outbreaks of violence, mainly in localised areas of Northern Ireland, known as 'The Troubles'. This unhappy era began when a civil rights march by Catholics in Derry was attacked by the Royal Ulster Constabulary (the police force) and loyalists (those loyal to the

---

DON'T LEAVE IRELAND WITHOUT...

Drinking in a traditional pub. You haven't experienced Ireland until you've nursed a pint of Guinness while listening to traditional Irish music. Head north of the border, though, for our pick of the pubs: Belfast's Crown Liquor Saloon with its ornate Victorian interior. See page 94.

Kissing the Blarney Stone. Even if it doesn't bestow the 'gift of the gab', it's a dizzying experience. See page 56.

Shopping for Irish crafts. From Waterford crystal to fine linen, and Aran sweaters to traditional jewellery, Ireland is a shopper's paradise. See page 20.

Driving the Ring of Kerry. With stunning coastal and mountain views, this circular drive is simply world-class. See page 62.

Exploring Georgian Dublin. You can still glimpse the Dublin Mountains from the city's 18th-century Georgian squares, as you could when they were built. See page 36.

Walking along a deserted beach. Ireland is blessed with scores of long, sandy beaches. To find one that's empty, too, try counties Sligo and Donegal, in the northwest. See page 88.

A Connemara village

British Crown). The IRA intensified its 'armed struggle' in Northern Ireland, seeking the unification of the island under Irish administration. Between 1969 and 2001, 3,526 people were killed in the struggle, about two thirds of them civilians. Eventually a compromise was reached, in which the Republic amended its constitution to abandon its claims of sovereignty over Northern Ireland and the IRA agreed to lay down its arms. Elected Protestant and Republican leaders agreed to enter a power-sharing assembly at Stormont in Belfast, and work together for the good of Northern Ireland.

Economics

The Republic suffered badly from the world economic downturn in 2008 and from revelations of dubious practices among bankers and property developers, the bill for which was passed to the taxpayer. Since 2014, however, the economy has rallied – with widespread growth and a robust increase in property prices – and the tourist industry continues to flourish, with record visitor numbers in 2016.

A WARM WELCOME

While nobody goes to Ireland for the weather, and the prices may not be cheap, the country has managed to combine modern comforts and traditional hospitality in an attractive way. The people have an outstanding capacity for fun, and have retained a natural courtesy and friendliness that has disappeared elsewhere. When asked what they like best about Ireland, for most visitors the answer is 'the Irish people'.

Irish literature

The Irish love telling stories, and listening to them too. Before the written word, travelling storytellers *(seanchaí)* entertained beside the fireside. The tradition of impromptu verbal wit lives on with Irish comedians and broadcasters. English spoken and written in Ireland differs from English elsewhere, with echoes of Irish-language words and constructions persisting. Jonathan Swift (1667–1745), satirist and author of *Gulliver's Travels*, and dramatist Oscar Wilde (1854–1900) are among the Irish writers whose works continue to be enjoyed worldwide. For a small country, Ireland has an impressive roster of winners of the Nobel Prize for Literature: George Bernard Shaw (1856–1950), W.B. Yeats (1865–1939), Samuel Beckett (1906–89) and Seamus Heaney (1939–2013). Literary festivals are convivial, informal events, where authors and the reading public mingle freely. The biggest one of all is Bloomsday (16 June), a four-day event that commemorates James Joyce's *Ulysses* (1922) in its Dublin setting (see www.bloomsdayfestival.ie).

Café in Kinvara   *Enjoying a pint in Dublin*

TOP TIPS FOR EXPLORING IRELAND

Newgrange. Newgrange (www.newgrange. com), a large Neolithic tomb in the Boyne Valley near Drogheda north of Dublin, looks like a man-made hilltop, but is in fact an amazing feat of prehistoric engineering and one of Europe's best examples of a passage-grave. The narrow tunnel leading to the central shrine is positioned to let the sun shine in on the shortest day of the year, 21 December. At its end you can stand in the circular vault and look up at the ceiling to see the remarkable 5,000-year-old technique used in its construction.

National Library. Those with an interest in Irish literature should visit Dublin's National Library of Ireland (2/3 Kildare Street; www.nli.ie). The library's changing exhibitions draw on its vast resources; look out for manuscripts, letters and first editions of Irish writers such as W.B. Yeats and James Joyce.

Joyce Centre. Also in Dublin, fans may wish to make a detour to the James Joyce Centre (35 North Great George's Street; www.jamesjoyce.ie), which showcases editions of Joyce's works, reconstructs his living quarters and displays some of his letters to Nora Barnacle, leaving out the seamier details. The Centre also organises lectures, 'Bloomsday' events (commemorating 16 June 1904, the day in which the events of Ulysses unfold) and walking tours of the city.

Wexford. County Wexford borders Wicklow to the north, Kilkenny to the west and Waterford to the south. Its long coastline to the east has many sandy beaches. If you are arriving by car at Rosslare, Wexford town, 18km (11 miles) northwest of the ferry terminal, makes a pleasant stop. It consists of a series of quays parallel to the water and a main street one block inland, with small, old-fashioned shops and pubs. At Ferrycarrig, 5km (3 miles) northwest of Wexford town on the N11, is the Irish National Heritage Park (www.inhp.com). This open-air museum on the banks of the River Slaney provides a useful introduction to Ireland's history and architecture from Stone Age man (6,000BC) to the arrival of the Normans in the 12th century.

Blasket Island Trips. At the tip of the Dingle Peninsula is Dunquin Pier, a steep concrete footpath that spirals down to the sea. A modern ferry (www.blasket islands.ie) makes the 20-minute crossing to Great Blasket Island, weather permitting, a number of times a day between Easter and October. Walk through the island's deserted village and along narrow cliff paths rich in wildlife, and watch the seals on White Strand.

Titanic Belfast. To explore the history of the RMS *Titanic* and its doomed 1912 voyage, go to the Titanic Belfast visitor centre (www.titanicbelfast.com). Nicknamed 'the iceberg' by locals, this 12,000-sq-metre (130,000-sq-ft) aluminium-clad building is the same height as the *Titanic*'s prow and occupies the Harland & Wolf shipyard where the *Titanic* was built.

Oysters fresh from the Atlantic

FOOD AND DRINK

Ireland has an abundance of farm-fresh produce and sea-fresh fish, but only recently has a distinctive style of Irish cooking emerged. A new generation of chefs are creating an exciting new dining experience at all price levels.

Traditionally, Irish food was plain but hearty. Bread and potatoes accompanied the main meal; a meat stew if you were lucky, or fish on Fridays. Vegetables were boiled to a pulp and salads were a rare summer treat. Garlic, avocados and aubergines were unheard of in most homes. However, in one generation Irish cooking has changed beyond all recognition. There is a new awareness of the amazing raw materials available to chefs in the form of grass-fed beef and lamb, fresh seafood from the Atlantic, abundant dairy produce and home-grown vegetables and salads. Even the humble Irish soda bread, made without yeast or other additives, and once considered inferior to shop-bought white bread, has come to be valued for its health-giving wholesomeness. Try a classic treat of six raw oysters, soda bread and half a pint of black stout to understand its appeal.

LOCAL CUISINE

Ireland's high-quality produce is imaginatively prepared by today's chefs to emphasise its freshness, flavour and texture. Ireland's chefs work closely with artisan food producers, who use traditional methods to smoke fish and make charcuterie and farmhouse cheeses. Many restaurants grow their own salads and herbs, or have an arrangement with a local grower. When people eat out, they have come to expect a high standard of cuisine, whether at an expensive restaurant or at the local café.

Irish chefs are trained in the classic tradition, and most go abroad for a few years and bring back culinary influences from their travels – generally Mediterranean, but sometimes eastern – adapting them to the Irish market. This eclectic approach is also followed by Ireland's private cookery schools, the best known being Ballymaloe Cookery School near the famous country house hotel. Darina Allen, its director, has been preaching the doctrine of using fresh local produce, treated with simplicity and respect, since 1983, and has trained many of today's Irish chefs.

Traditional favourites

The fondness for the potato continues to be a national stereotype. The humble 'spud' will often be served in three different ways – mashed, chipped and dauphinoise, for example. Many Irish

Stout and soda bread

Fresh produce at a farmers' market

people like to order steak when they eat out, and it will be found on even the fanciest of menus.

Many people also eat their main meal – known as dinner – at midday. Pubs advertising 'carvery lunches' offer two or three roast meats carved to order at a self-service counter, with a selection of traditional vegetables, and, of course, spuds. Another favourite is fish and chips, traditionally eaten as a takeaway in the street, but now served even in the most upmarket restaurants, like Kinsale's Fishy Fishy. Bread (served with butter on the side) has become a star turn in Irish restaurants, with most places baking their own or buying it in from a specialist bakery.

Farm to fork

All meat in Ireland is now traceable back to the farm, and the flavour of locally

Coffee the Irish way and the Italian way

reared and butchered meat comes as a pleasant surprise. The Irish Food Board runs a programme, Féile Bia, encouraging restaurants to source as much as possible of their food locally and pass on the information about its provenance to their customers. 'Bia' is the Irish word for food, and 'féile' means both festival and celebration. These words on the menu mean that the restaurant is committed to serving carefully sourced fresh local produce. This will often be game in the autumn and winter, such as venison, pheasant, duck and woodcock.

Farmers' markets

Farmers' markets, where producers sell directly to the public, are a great addition to the Irish food scene. They are ideal for picnic food, offering local farmhouse cheeses, charcuterie and patés. Traditional breads and baking are also a strong point, as are jams, chutneys and sauces, and fresh organic salads, fruit and vegetables. Check out www.irish farmersmarkets.ie.

WHERE TO EAT

Fine dining

Some 50 years ago, there were hardly any restaurants in Ireland apart from hotel dining rooms, especially in provincial towns. Even today, some of the best restaurants are still to be found in hotels, such as the Park Hotel Kenmare on the Ring of Kerry. Even in Dublin, hotel restaurants are chic, none more so

Irish oatmeal fishcake

than the Cleaver East at the U2-owned Clarence Hotel. Many hotels have two or more restaurants, one for fine dining and another informal. They also have the advantage of being open daily, whereas many Irish restaurants close after Sunday lunch and do not serve dinner on Sunday or Monday. Booking is advisable at most restaurants, but even the best, like Dublin's top places – Restaurant Patrick Guilbaud, Chapter One, Thorntons and L'Ecrivain – are relatively informal, specifying only 'smart casual' at dinner. If you want to treat yourself, remember that lunch is generally less expensive than dinner. Restaurants often have special-value 'early bird' menus for diners who arrive before 7 or 7.30pm.

Bistros, wine bars and brasseries

The Irish have an idiosyncratic way with these terms, all of which can be interpreted as an 'informal, fun place without tablecloths'. A high rate of VAT and high overheads make it very difficult to run a stylish and good-value establishment, but people do try, like Bloom Brasserie on Baggot St, Dublin, the Chart House in Dingle town or the White Gable Restaurant in Moycullen. An increasingly popular way of keeping prices down is to offer a tapas menu, where dishes can be shared, such as the Market Bar in Dublin. Northern Ireland can be better value, especially if the pound is weak; in Belfast seek out the brasseries along Botanic Avenue for good-quality food at student-friendly prices.

Pubs

Since the introduction of the smoking ban and drink-driving laws, pubs have had to diversify. Nearly everywhere now serves tea and coffee, and espresso machines are commonplace in city pubs. More are serving food, often with an all-day menu that may feature soups, sandwiches, salads and a couple of hot dishes, or at a self-service 'carvery'. The best pub food is found in places that offer daily specials at lunchtime and in the early evening, like The Locke Bar in Limerick city. Most pubs stop serving food at around 9pm, to make more room for drinkers. Some pubs, like Vaughan's Anchor Inn in Liscannor, have effectively turned into restaurants that also serve drinks, with waiter service at all tables. Others, like Moran's Oyster Cottage in Kilcolgan, have a separate restaurant area with a full menu. Children are welcome in most food-serving pubs in the daytime, and some even have play areas and children's menus.

Daytime cafés

Since the Irish acquired a taste for real coffee, cafés have bucked up no end. They usually offer some form of home-baking, often the ubiquitous scone or a warm slice of quiche, as well as sandwiches, salads and home-made soups, and perhaps a pasta option.

Oysters in Kinsale

Irish scones

DRINKS

Irish pubs are expensive. A pint of beer in Dublin will set you back between €5–€6 (compared to about €3.80 in a rural pub), and a soft drink can cost €4–€5. Wine by the glass goes from about €4.50 in a country pub to €8 or more in a fancy Dublin hotel. Try to be philosophical: you are not just paying for the drink, you are paying for the experience of being in a real Irish pub. With any luck, you will get some free live music (most likely after 10pm), or some witty conversation.

Irish stout

Irish pubs sell the usual range of beer and lager, bottled and on tap, in measures of a pint or half pint, but the one that every visitor has to try is stout, a strongish black beer with a creamy white head. Murphy's is brewed in Cork, but the most famous stout is Guinness, which has been brewed in Dublin since 1759. Great care is taken in serving it; about half a glass is poured and left to 'settle' for several minutes, then topped with the trademark creamy head. In a good Irish pub it will taste smooth as velvet, bearing no relation to the Guinness served in Britain or America.

Irish whiskey

It is spelt differently from Scotch 'whisky' and tastes different too, as it is distilled from a mixture of malted and unmalted barley grains. Irish whiskey has seen a huge resurgence in recent years, with popular newcomers such as Kilbeggan Distillery in County Westmeath and Dingle Distillery in County Kerry, although the old favourites of Bushmills, Jameson and Paddy are still the market leaders, and all have a slightly different flavour. The fine old single malts are generally taken neat or with a splash of water as a digestif. Irish whiskey is also used in Irish coffee, a hot, sweet coffee spiked with whiskey and topped with cream, a delicious way to end a meal.

If you have spent too long in the cold outdoors, there is no better cure than a hot whiskey, ideally sipped in front of an open fire. The bartender should dissolve a teaspoon of sugar in about an inch of boiling hot water, adding a slice of lemon studded with cloves and, of course, a measure of whiskey. Add more hot water to taste, and feel the warmth spreading to the very core of your being.

Food and Drink Prices

Price guide for a two-course dinner for one in the Republic of Ireland:
€€€€ = over 40 euros
€€€ = 30–40 euros
€€ = 20–30 euros
€ = under 20 euros
Price guide for a two-course dinner for one in Northern Ireland:
££££ = over £40
£££ = £25–40
££ = £15–25
£ = under £15

Irish whiskey

SHOPPING

Shopping in the two capitals is a pleasant experience, as both have compact centres. Designers use Irish wool and tweeds in high-fashion lines, while traditional craftmakers offer heirloom quality in glass, ceramics, linen and wool.

Both Dublin and Belfast have lively shopping areas, with a mix of department stores, high-street chains and quirky boutiques. In addition, there are shops that sell primarily Irish-made fashion and homewares, which attract Irish buyers as well as visitors. Cork, Limerick and Galway, and smaller towns like Kilkenny, Waterford and Tralee, have shops within the historic centres, so you can combine cultural tourism with retail therapy. Outside the cities, look out for craft shops and galleries with jewellery, leather, ceramics, glass, candles and prints.

DUBLIN

Shops north of the river are generally less fashionable but better value than those to the south. British chain stores Marks & Spencer, Debenhams and Boots are prevalent. Ireland's version of Marks & Spencer is Dunnes Stores, while Irish-owned Penney's (Primark in the UK) is a mecca for bargain hunters. Brown Thomas on Grafton Street is an up-market department store for lovers of Chanel, Louis Vuitton et al; it also has branches in Cork, Limerick and Galway.

North of the river

O'Connell Street is Dublin's main thoroughfare, with plenty of shops and attractions. It is home to historic – and sadly now closed down – Clerys, founded in 1853 as one of the world's first department stores and under whose iconic clock generations of Dubliners have met. From O'Connell Street, Henry Street runs past the famous Moore Street Market, where colourful characters sell fruit and vegetables with razor-sharp patter. It leads to the Ilac Centre, a large shopping centre, and the Jervis Centre. The recently revamped Arnotts department store, now owned by Selfridges of London, is also well worth a look-in.

South of the river

No doubt about it, the pedestrianised Grafton Street that runs from Trinity College south to St Stephen's Green is a great deal of fun, renowned for its buskers and street performers. Do not miss the Powerscourt Townhouse Centre to the west, an 18th-century mansion converted into a stylish shopping complex, and the massive glass-roofed Stephen's Green Shopping Centre (with an enor-

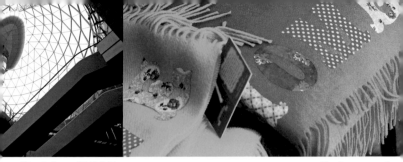

Victoria Square Mall, Belfast   *Hand-woven wool*

mous branch of Dunnes). Grafton Street is a haven for fashionistas, with cat-walk-inspired fashion for every budget.

To the west and northwest of Grafton Street, moving towards Temple Bar, you will find streetwear stores and music shops. Nassau Street near Trinity College has a branch of the Kilkenny Shop (Irish crafts and design), and there is a large branch of Avoca Handweavers in Suffolk Street. For Irish ladies' fashion, go to the first floor of Brown Thomas. Nassau Street, Dawson Street and Duke Street are rich in bookshops.

CORK, LIMERICK, GALWAY AND SLIGO

Patrick Street is Cork city's mainstream shopping area, with more interesting boutiques, bookshops and galleries in Paul Street. Limerick's main drag is O'Connell Street; just off it is lively, pedestrianised Cruises Street. Besides its long main street, Galway has two large shopping malls near Eyre Square for more everyday stuff. Revamped Sligo town has an impressive shopping centre, the Quayside, between Lower Quay Street and Wine Street.

BELFAST

Belfast has a bewildering choice of shops and, since you pay in sterling, they are often much better value than their southern neighbours. The most recent addition is the Victoria Square Shopping Centre, with its flagship House of Fraser department store, but Royal Avenue and the CastleCourt Centre are also worth a visit. Meanwhile, Botanic Avenue and the Queen's Quarter are filled with quirky bookshops, organic delis and vintage fashion boutiques. The Lisburn Road, to the south, is the destination for designer clothes and chichi home stores.

WHAT TO BUY

Hand-made crafts are expensive, and you will want to spend some time over your decision, but that is part of the fun. Shop around as you travel, comparing prices and quality. Kilkenny is a good place to start; Kilkenny Design Centre opposite the castle will give you an idea of the high quality and scope of what is on offer, such as hand-made ceramics, hand-loomed mohair or alpaca blankets, fine linen that will last a lifetime and crystal glass, traditionally cut or in modern designs (Jerpoint Glass is superb). Irish-made jewellery also comes in traditional styles (Galway's Claddagh ring, for example). Then there are sweaters and other knitted goods that make good presents. Tweed is made in Connemara and Donegal, and you can still buy hand-knitted sweaters on the Aran Islands, with a label naming the knitter. As well as Kilkenny, you will find a good range of craft shops in Avoca, Blarney, Kinsale, Kenmare, Dingle, Clifden and Westport.

Irish dancing

ENTERTAINMENT

Ireland's reputation as an easy-going party-loving nation is reflected in a packed calendar of arts and music festivals. Dublin is the theatre capital, while traditional music and dance can be found in every corner of the land.

The unexpected success of the Wexford Festival Opera – where international stars attracted large audiences to a small port in southeast Ireland, performing lesser-known operas in the dank Irish October – inspired an ambitious annual calendar of festivals and events. As in Wexford, these provide a buzz for the local community, with plenty of free entertainment, while also attracting visitors and boosting the local economy. While Ireland continues to maintain a high profile internationally in the literary and theatrical world, it also has the dubious kudos of being the originator of one of the world's most successful dance spectaculars, *Riverdance* (1994), responsible for making Irish dancing sexy. For entertainment and nightlife listings, see the Directory.

THEATRE

Ever since the Abbey Theatre's production of *The Playboy of the Western World* by John M. Synge in 1907 caused a famous riot (people reacted violently to its use of the word 'shift', referring to a female undergarment), Dublin has had an exciting theatre scene. It also

offers great value for money, with tickets at the Abbey starting at €15, often available at short notice. Productions from the Gate Theatre, which fostered the work of Brian Friel, regularly transfer to New York.

Belfast, Wexford, Kilkenny, Waterford, Cork, Galway and Sligo all have well-equipped theatres that host touring productions and sometimes produce their own too. Galway's Druid Theatre Company has successfully transferred productions to Broadway, such as Martin McDonagh's *The Cripple of Inishman*.

Language is no barrier at Siamsa Tíre, Ireland's National Folk Theatre (Town Park, Tralee, Co. Kerry; www.siamsatire.com). The titles of the plays are Irish, and the themes are based on Celtic myth and folklore, but the performances are energetic spectaculars, featuring music, song, dance and mime, with no dialogue.

DANCE

Before *Riverdance* burst on to the scene, very few traditional Irish dancers made a living by toe-tapping. Now tour-

Temple Bar, Dublin   *Fiddler in Belfast*

ing productions are in great demand, and can also be seen in Irish cabaret at places like Bunratty Castle and the Arlington Hotel on Bachelor's Walk in Dublin. The best way to enjoy Irish dance is to join in a set dancing session; these are like the barn or square dances. Set dancing sessions take place in pubs and community halls, and newcomers are usually welcomed and taught a few steps.

MUSIC

Wherever you travel in Ireland you will encounter live traditional music, most often in a pub. A gathering of traditional musicians on an informal, unpaid basis is known as a *seisiún* (session), and creates its own momentum, as musicians improvise and take flight. Many publicans employ musicians to entertain their customers from about 10pm, and the music is usually free.

NIGHTLIFE

Dublin has more than 120 clubs and live-music pubs. The club scene is mainly for the under 35s, who flock to the city from all over Europe in search of a good time. In the rest of the Republic, nightlife is generally an extension of the pub scene; quite literally, as certain pubs in each town are regularly granted a special licence, known as an extension, to stay open until 2am. Ask locally.

In Belfast you can find traditional city-centre music venues, a burgeoning bar scene in the Cathedral Quarter and shabby-chic music clubs in the student areas of the south.

Festivals

The festival season opens with Dublin's five-day celebration of St Patrick's Day on 17 March. It was originally introduced because so many visitors were disappointed to find that, unlike the shenanigans abroad, nothing much happened in Ireland on the great day.

Festivals are now a key element in Ireland's entertainment scene. An Irish festival often goes on for a 10-day 'week', including weekends, and aims to entertain all, from children to the elderly. You never know who you will find headlining the list of attractions: a 'local' like Van Morrison or Sinead O'Connor, or a big-name guest from the shores beyond. Cork Midsummer Festival (June), Galway Arts Festival (July), Kilkenny Arts Festival (August) and Belfast International Arts Festival (October) are among the biggest general arts fests. Popular newcomers include the City Spectacular in Dublin and Cork (July), and Galway's Baboró International Arts Festival for Children (October). There are also specialist festivals for classical music and traditional music (known as *fleadh*), and literary festivals galore.

Golf is hugely popular

ACTIVITIES

Ireland has long been a destination for lovers of the outdoors. Initially attracting golfers and anglers, its easily accessible wilderness areas now lure walkers, climbers and cyclists, while its beaches have been discovered by surfers.

Ireland's golf courses continue to be a major magnet for visitors, its traditional links courses now joined by major new developments. Meanwhile, game, coarse and sea anglers are hooked by Ireland's network of lakes and rivers and long coastline. Walkers are catered for by a range of looped and waymarked walks, cyclists can follow sign-posted trails and surfers can make the most of the Atlantic swell. See www.discoverireland.ie.

GOLFING

Ireland has more than 400 courses around the island, including over 30 percent of the world's natural links courses. The Irish are keen golfers, and it is generally seen as an accessible sport of the people, rather than a status symbol. The majority of Irish clubs are unstuffy places that welcome visitors, who are usually pleasantly surprised at the low price of green fees. Exceptions to this are the more expensive parkland courses at the K-Club, Adare Manor and Mount Juliet, and some of the more famous links courses like Lahinch and Waterville. See www.golf.discoverireland.ie.

ANGLING

The infrastructure of angling centres and boat operators has improved greatly in recent years. Alas, at the same time, water quality has declined all over Ireland. While the old-timers will tell you that the fishing is not what it used to be, Ireland continues to be a popular destination for game, coarse and sea angling.

WALKING

There are now 44 long-distance waymarked walking routes, and a network of shorter looped walks, designed so that you return to your starting point within one to three hours. It is easy to escape the crowds in such a sparsely populated country, and you can be walking in impressively wild, uninhabited scenery within an hour or less of landing at the airport. To find a nearby walk see www.irishtrails.ie.

CYCLING

Certain towns, such as Westport, Achill, Skibbereen and Clifden have been designated 'cycling hubs', as they pro-

Surfing off the west coast   *Horse-riding in Connemara*

vide good accommodation and eating options, along with a choice of looped cycling routes suitable for all fitness levels. Organised cycling holidays are increasingly popular, either travelling in a group with a back-up van, or cycling independently to pre-booked accommodation, with baggage transfer. There are also designated mountain-bike parks on forest tracks in rural areas for adrenaline addicts. See www.cyclingireland.ie.

HORSE-RIDING

Ireland rears some of the world's finest horses, from million-dollar racehorses to good-natured, long-haired ponies. Whether you choose a residential riding holiday with tuition on a challenging cross-country course, or a pleasant amble around quiet lanes on a hairy pony, be honest about your abilities, so that the stable can match you with the right horse. See www.ehi.ie.

ADVENTURE CENTRES

Learn sea-kayaking, canoeing, orienteering, rock climbing, abseiling and other outdoor skills at the network of outdoor adventure centres. Send the kids, or book a guided family day out.

SURFING

Beaches used to be empty in bad weather, except for a few dog walkers. Now they are busy whatever the weather, with wake-boarders, kitesurfers, windsurfers and, most numerous of all, surfers. A wetsuit is essential, but it is a rare day when you will not find a rideable wave on the west coast. Surf schools offer tuition to beginners on the more benign beach breaks, while the more advanced surfers are towed out by jet-ski, hoping to catch the famous Aileen's wave beneath the Cliffs of Moher, home to some of Europe's biggest waves at over 7.5 metres (25 feet) – awesome! See www.irishsurfing.ie.

Gaelic games

Hurling and Gaelic football arouse such passions in Ireland that they are often described as a religion. These are fast-paced, high-voltage games, played by dedicated amateurs, organised around the local parish and controlled by the Gaelic Athletic Association (GAA). Hurling is played with a wooden hurley, which can propel the ball along the ground, carry the ball aloft on its paddle-like extreme or throw it in the air. It is said to be one of the fastest ball games in the world, and is certainly one of the most exciting to watch. Gaelic football, like hurling, is played by teams of 15-a-side, on the same size pitch, with a round, football-sized ball. It has similarities with rugby and football. Throwing is not allowed. The main season runs from early summer, and culminates in the All-Ireland finals in Dublin's Croke Park in late September. For fixtures, see www.gaa.ie.

Carrowmore Megalithic Cemetery, Co. Sligo

HISTORY: KEY DATES

Ireland has changed from a traditional post-colonial society to a secular, multiracial one, and is weathering the transition from economic boom to almost-bust and back again. But the Irish maintain their reputation for knowing how to have fun.

EARLY PERIOD

c.7,000BC	Date of earliest archaeological evidence found along the coast.
500BC	Celts migrate to Britain. Ireland's Iron Age begins.
432AD	St Patrick arrives as a missionary.
500–800	Early monasticism; Ireland becomes a European learning centre.
9th century	The Vikings invade, founding Dublin.
1014	Brian Ború, King of Munster, defeats the Vikings.

ENGLISH CONQUEST

1169	The Anglo-Normans conquer large areas of the island.
1541	Henry VIII declares himself King of Ireland.
1606	Plantation of Ulster brings English and Scottish Protestant settlers.
1649	Irish Catholic rebellions are viciously crushed by Oliver Cromwell.
1690	William of Orange wins Battle of the Boyne; Protestant rule begins.
1691	The Irish-Protestant parliament introduces the 'Penal Laws' denying Catholics the right to hold public office, own property or vote.

FREEDOM STRUGGLES

1798	Wolfe Tone's Rebellion is crushed by the British; 30,000 die.
1801	Ireland incorporated into the United Kingdom by the Act of Union.
1829	Daniel O'Connell achieves Catholic Emancipation.
1845–9	The Great Famine results in the deaths of around 1 million.
1858	IRA forerunner the Irish Republican Brotherhood is founded.
1875	Charles Stewart Parnell elected MP; leads Home Rule movement.
1885	Home Rule is defeated in the House of Lords.
1905–12	The struggle over Home Rule intensifies with the formation of armed militias, including the Ulster Volunteer Force.

Irish Civil War procession

INDEPENDENCE AND AFTER

1916	The Easter Rising is defeated and martial law imposed.
1918	Sinn Féin wins the general election, boycotts the House of Commons and elects the jailed Eamon de Valera as president.
1919–21	Irish War of Independence between the British Army and the IRA.
1921	Britain and Ireland sign a treaty granting 'Dominion' status to Ireland. The six counties of Ulster remain in UK.
1922–3	The Irish Civil War between pro- and anti-partitionists.
1937	The Constitution of Ireland comes into effect, asserting the national sovereignty of the Irish people.
1939–45	During World War II the Irish Free State remains neutral.
1949	Irish Free State leaves the Commonwealth, becoming a Republic.

NORTH AND SOUTH RECONCILE

1969	A civil rights dispute in Northern Ireland leads to the armed struggle known as 'The Troubles'.
1972	14 civilians shot dead by security forces at a civil rights march on 'Bloody Sunday'.
1973	Ireland joins the European Community (now the European Union).
1990	Mary Robinson is elected the Republic's first woman president.
1998	All parties sign the Northern Ireland peace treaty known as the Good Friday Agreement.
1999	All-party assembly with limited powers set up in Northern Ireland.
2002	The Republic adopts the euro. In the North, direct rule from London is imposed.
2003	Elections in Northern Ireland restore the all-party assembly.

MODERN IRELAND

2004	Ireland's economic boom, the 'Celtic Tiger', is at its peak.
2005	The IRA says its war is over, its weapons destroyed.
2008	Global financial crisis. Years of recession ensue.
2013	Abortion legalised in medical emergencies.
2015	Same-sex marriage legalised in the Republic.
2016	Enda Kenny's Fine Gael party forms a minority government.

BEST ROUTES

St Patrick's Cathedral

HISTORIC DUBLIN

This full-day route covers the main historic sights of Dublin, skirting the banks of the River Liffey and taking in the medieval centre, Trinity College and Temple Bar, one of the oldest – and liveliest – parts of the city.

DISTANCE: 5.25km (3.25 miles)
TIME: A full day
START: Four Courts
END: Clarence Hotel, Temple Bar
POINTS TO NOTE: To reach the starting point, take the tram (Luas) to the Four Courts stop, just behind the Four Courts Building. If you intend to visit most or all of the sights on this route, consider buying a Dublin Pass. The pass will give you free entry to most major Dublin attractions (see www.dublinpass.ie for details of where you can buy this). On Sundays Dublin Castle is only open in the afternoon.

Although Mesolithic and Neolithic peoples occupied settlements in the area in the 8th century BC, it was not until the Vikings arrived in the 9th century AD that Dublin first came into existence. In the winter of 841 the Vikings settled on the banks of the River Liffey. Following the Anglo-Norman invasion of 1169, the Normans built Dublin Castle, and the cathedrals of St Patrick and Christchurch. This route begins in the very area where the Vikings and later the Normans set down their roots in Dublin.

The modern Irish Gaelic name for Dublin, 'Baile Átha Cliath', first recorded in 1368, translates as 'Town of the Ford of the Reed Hurdles'. It refers to a fording point of the Liffey near Heuston Station, to the west of Father Mathew Bridge.

FOUR COURTS

Begin at the **Four Courts ❶** on Inns Quay, on the northern side of the river. Notable for its large dome and portico, the building was designed between 1796 and 1802 by James Gandon (who also designed the Custom House, further east down the river, and the Bank of Ireland). The name is derived from the four divisions that traditionally constituted the Irish judicial system: Chancery, King's Bench, Exchequer and Common Pleas; this remains the main court building for the Irish Republic.

Cross over the Liffey at the **Father Mathew Bridge**. Looking left towards

Four Courts dome

the city centre, the southern riverbank leads from Merchants Quay to Wood Quay, the site of the first Viking settlement in what is now the city centre. The settlement was actually sited on the River Poddle, a tributary of the Liffey; however, it was covered up in the late 1700s and largely forgotten.

SOUTH OF THE RIVER

Crossing onto Bridge Street, you will pass the **Brazen Head**, which claims to be Ireland's oldest pub (established in 1198). From here the road bends left to meet Cornmarket, where you will pass the two **churches of St Audoen**: on the left, the 19th-century Catholic church; on the right, a Church of Ireland edifice, built in 1190. The latter, Dublin's only surviving medieval church, is thought to be the oldest of its kind in Ireland. Facing them is the **Tailors' Hall** (1706), Dublin's only remaining guildhall.

St Patrick's Cathedral

Continuing along Cornmarket onto High Street, a right turn takes you down Nicholas Street to **St Patrick's Cathedral ❷** (St Patrick's Close; www.stpatrickscathedral.ie; Mar–Oct Mon–Fri 9.30am–5pm, Sat 9am–6pm, Sun 9–10.30am, 12.30–2.30pm, 4.30–6pm, Nov–Feb Mon–Sat 9.30am–5pm, Sun 9–10.30am, 12.30–2.30pm, with exceptions). A church has

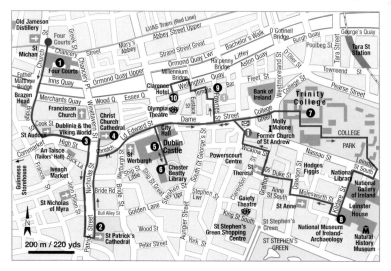

Dublin Castle

stood here since the 5th century, while legend has it that St Patrick baptised converts at a well in the churchyard. The present cathedral was built by the Normans and restored in the mid-19th century; particularly impressive are the enormous flying buttresses that support the magnificent roof. Jonathan Swift, the Dublin-born author of *Gulliver's Travels* and master of prose satire, was Dean here between 1714 and 1745. The well-manicured cathedral gardens are free to visit.

Christchurch Place

Retrace your steps along Nicholas Street to **Dublinia and the Viking World** ❸ (St Michael's Hill; www.dublinia.ie; Mar–Sept daily 10am–6.30pm, Oct–Feb until 5.30pm), just past High Street on the left. Reconstructions of medieval street scenes, gory exhibitions of medieval medicine and torture, and interactive presentations of Viking life will keep kids entertained for hours.

Opposite are the gardens of **Christ Church Cathedral** ❹ (Christchurch Place; www.christchurchdublin.ie; Apr–Sept Mon–Sat 9.30am–7pm, Sun 12.30–2.30pm, 4.30–7pm, Mar, Oct Mon–Sat 9.30am–6pm, Sun 12.30–2.30pm, 4.30–6pm, Nov–Feb Mon–Sat 9.30am–5pm, Sun 12.30–2.30pm). Begun in about 1030, Christchurch is the only cathedral of Norse foundation in Ireland or Britain. It was rebuilt in Norman times and remodelled in the 1870s. Highlights include the beautiful

tiled floor and the 11th-century crypt, the oldest structure in Dublin.

At the end of Christchurch Place, cross over Werburgh Street and take the left of the two facing roads – Lord Edward Street. At the point at which Lord Edward Street meets Dame Street, a right turn just before the **City Hall** (built in 1769) will take you to Cork Hill, and the bright red facade of **The Queen of Tarts**, one of the city's best cafés.

DUBLIN CASTLE

Cork Hill Gate is the official entrance to **Dublin Castle** ❺ (Castle Street; www.dublincastle.ie; daily 9.45am–5.15pm; grounds free; entrance to State apartments by 45-min guided tour). Historical evidence suggests that a Danish Viking fortress was built here in around 930AD. The Normans built a wood-and-stone castle in the 1170s; then, between 1204 and 1230, King John erected a larger, stronger castle on the same site. Unfortunately, most of the medieval castle, except for the south-eastern tower, was destroyed by fire in 1684. As it stands today, the majority of the castle dates from the Georgian era. Tours of the castle take in the grand State Apartments, the Gothic-Revivalist Chapel Royal and the fascinating medieval Undercroft, the point at which the city walls join the castle below ground.

Follow the signs through the castle grounds to the **Castle Gardens**, site of the first 'pool' of the city – the 'Dubh-

Christ Church door knocker   *Tiled floor of the cathedral*

linn' ('black pool') from which the city derives its name. The Vikings would moor their ships at this spot, where the River Poddle 'pooled'.

Chester Beatty Library

Continuing through the Castle Gardens takes you to the magnificently quirky **Chester Beatty Library** ❻ (Dublin Castle; www.cbl.ie; Mon–Fri 10am–5pm, Sat 11am–5pm, Sun 1–5pm, Oct–Apr closed Mon; free). Permanent exhibitions, taken from the extensive collections of the American mining magnate and art patron Sir Alfred Chester Beatty (1875–1968), include Islamic, Christian, Jewish and Buddhist manuscripts, printed texts, religious artefacts and artworks. There is also a pleasant roof garden, a reading room and a bookshop. The excellent **Silk Road Café**, in the atrium on the ground floor, echoes the museum's eastern leanings.

TRINITY COLLEGE

Leave the castle grounds by Cork Hill Gate and turn right onto Dame Street, which leads straight down to **College Green**, a popular meeting spot.

College Green faces the 18th-century Irish Houses of Parliament, which now house the **Bank of Ireland**, completed in 1785 by James Gandon (open during banking hours). A **statue of Henry Grattan** (1746–1820), the Irish parliament's greatest orator, stands in the middle of the green.

Trinity College ❼ was founded in 1592 by Elizabeth I on the site of a confiscated monastery. Established to educate the Protestant Ascendancy class, Trinity College has educated a host of Anglo-Irish cultural figures. Famous alumni include the historian and statesman Edmund Burke, writer Oliver Goldsmith, and poet Thomas Moore, and more recently Oscar Wilde, playwright J.M. Synge and Bram Stoker, author of *Dracula*.

The Front Gate was built between 1755 and 1759. Passing through it, you will reach the cobbled quadrangle of **Parliament Square**, with its tall (30 metre/100ft) campanile, designed by Sir Charles Lanyon and erected in 1853. On the right-hand side of Parliament Square is a little booth from where you can buy tickets for student-led tours of the College, including the Old Library and the *Book of Kells*.

Trinity College Library

Leaving Parliament Square by the top right corner, you will find (on your left) the entrance to **Trinity College Library** and the ***Book of Kells*** (www.tcd.ie/library/bookofkells; May–Sept Mon–Sat 8.30am–5pm, Sun 9.30–5pm, Oct–Apr Mon–Sat 9.30am–5pm, Sun noon–4.30pm). The *Book of Kells*, probably produced early in the 9th century by the monks of Iona, is one of the most beautifully illuminated manuscripts in the world. Its vellum pages contain the four Gospels in Latin, each one decorated with intricate painted illustrations.

Trinity College

The manuscript was given to Trinity College in the 17th century.

The **Old Library** (1712–32) contains the magnificent **Long Room**. Its high windows let in shafts of glorious light, which rest upon the high bookcases and on the busts of literary and artistic figures that flank them. Changing exhibitions from the library's collections are accompanied by a permanent display of one of the dozen remaining copies of the 1916 'Proclamation of the Irish Republic'.

Leaving the Old Library, turn left to enter the delightful **College Park**. Passing the cricket pavilion on your right, a right turn takes you to the southeastern exit of Trinity College.

KILDARE STREET AND DAWSON STREET

Turning right out of Trinity along Leinster Street South and taking the first left will bring you to Kildare Street, home of some of the most important buildings in Dublin. The first you will pass is the **National Library of Ireland** (1890) on your left. Next door is **Leinster House** (1746), seat of the two Oíreachtas (Houses of Parliament), the Dáil and the Seanad (Irish Parliament and Senate).

National Museum of Ireland

Like the National Library, the **National Museum of Ireland – Archaeology** ❽ (Kildare Street; www.museum.ie/Archaeology; Tue–Sat 10am–5pm, Sun 2–5pm; free) has a columnar entrance rotunda and was constructed in 1890. Its archaeological exhibitions trace the development of Irish civilisation from the Mesolithic or Middle Stone Age to Late Medieval Ireland; separate exhibitions also showcase artefacts from ancient Egypt and Cyprus. A visit to the museum is highly recommended, if only to marvel at its richly decorated interior.

Literary Dublin

Leaving Kildare Street west via Molesworth Street brings you to Dawson

---

Drinkers' Dublin

You can sample two of Ireland's most famous exports at locations near the city centre. The Guinness Brewery, 1km (0.6 mile) to the west, is the biggest brewery in Europe, producing 2.5 million pints of Guinness every day. The Guinness Storehouse (Thomas Street; www.guinnessstorehouse.com; daily 9.30am–7pm, July, Aug 9am–8pm) showcases the making and history of the world-famous stout. Admission entitles you to a complimentary pint in the Gravity Bar, the highest in Dublin, with panoramic views over the city.

Alternatively, the Old Jameson Distillery (Bow Street; www.tours.jameson whiskey.com) offers various whiskey experiences and is housed in the old warehouse of the 1791 whiskey factory.

Temple Bar graffiti

Street, home of the excellent **Hodges Figgis Bookshop** (56–8 Dawson Street). This elegant building contains an excellent selection of Irish literature and has a well-stocked 'bargain basement'. Meanwhile, **Ulysses Rare Books** (www.rarebooks.ie), selling rare books, prints and maps of Irish interest, can be found on nearby **Duke Street**, as well as the Duke Pub, starting point of Dublin's famous literary pub crawl (www.dublinpubcrawl.com).

Duke Street leads to the pedestrian shopping area of **Grafton Street**. A right turn takes you back towards College Green. Take the first left down **Wicklow Street**; you could recharge your batteries with a tasty vegetarian treat at **Cornucopia** (19–20 Wicklow Street; www.cornucopia.ie). Turn right from here and follow the bend into St Andrew Street to return to Dame Street.

TEMPLE BAR

Take any right turn off Dame Street (such as Fownes Street) to reach lively and chaotic **Temple Bar** ❾. The area is named after Sir William Temple, who acquired the land in the early 1600s; by the early 1700s it had become a place of ill repute, full of pubs and prostitutes. Today's Temple Bar still has the pubs, but the prostitutes have been replaced by artists, musicians and film-makers: the entire area was redeveloped when Dublin was selected as the 1991 European City of Culture.

Head through busy streets, avoiding the ubiquitous hen and stag parties, to arrive at the River Liffey. To the right is the white cast-iron arc of the 1816 **Ha'penny Bridge** (officially, the Liffey Bridge), one of Dublin's best-loved landmarks. The less exciting **Millennium Bridge**, to its left, joins Eustace Street in Temple Bar to the north quays.

On the south bank, west of the Millennium Bridge, is Wellington Quay, home of the **Clarence Hotel** ❿. Owned by Bono and the Edge from U2, the Clarence is the landmark building of Temple Bar. Built in 1852 and refurbished in Art Deco style, it stands on the site of Dublin's original Customs House. The Clarence's **Octagon Bar** is great for people watching over a pre-dinner cocktail. For dinner, a restaurant with a claim to fame of its own – Sinead O'Connor was once a waitress there – is nearby **Bad Ass Café**, see ❶.

Food and Drink

❶ BAD ASS CAFÉ

9–11 Crown Alley; tel: 01-675 3005; www.badassdublin.com; Sun–Thu 10am–late, Fri–Sat 8am–late; €€
This Dublin institution, where Sinead O'Connor once worked as a waitress, has been extensively refurbished but is still famous for its burgers. Great traditional Irish music.

MODERN DUBLIN

Modern Dublin was shaped by its writers, artists and thinkers. This route covers the literary, political and artistic sights of the city – from the Dublin Writers Museum to the General Post Office to the National Gallery of Ireland – to illustrate how Dublin became the culturally vibrant capital it is today.

DISTANCE: 4km (2.5 miles)
TIME: A full day
START: Parnell Square
END: National Gallery of Ireland
POINTS TO NOTE: Many city-centre buses pass close to the beginning of the route. Alternatively, Parnell Square is a 10-minute walk from Connolly and Tara Street DART stations, and a 5-minute walk north from the Abbey Street tram (Luas) stop. Note that Bewley's Café Theatre is closed on Sundays.

This route moves from north to south, taking in the inspirational Dublin Writers Museum and Dublin City Gallery The Hugh Lane on Parnell Square as well as the political and historical monuments of O'Connell Street and O'Connell Bridge, and passing into the fashionable southern side of the city, with its elegant shopping arcades, green spaces such as St Stephen's Green, and impressive Georgian architecture.

PARNELL SQUARE

Parnell Square, one of Dublin's five Georgian squares, is home to the **Garden of Remembrance** ❶ (daily 8.30am–6pm; free). Established in 1966 to commemorate the 50th anniversary of the 1916 Easter Rising, it is dedicated to the memory of all those who gave their lives for the cause of Irish freedom.

Dublin Writers Museum
Since 2010 Dublin has been designated a Unesco City of Literature in recognition of its literary heritage. A fine Georgian house on the north side of Parnell Square is home to the **Dublin Writers Museum** ❷ (18 Parnell Square North; www.writersmuseum.com; Mon–Sat 10am–5pm, Sun 11am–5pm). The museum chronicles the history of Irish writers and writing from its roots in poetry and storytelling to the 20th century, including Oscar Wilde, George Bernard Shaw, W.B. Yeats, James Joyce and Samuel Beckett. Right next door is the **Irish Writers Centre** (19 Parnell Square North; http://irishwriterscentre.

ie; Mon–Thu 10am–9pm, Fri until 5pm) which holds writing courses, talks, writing groups, book launches and readings.

Dublin City Gallery The Hugh Lane

A few doors down, the dazzling **Dublin City Gallery The Hugh Lane** ❸ (www.hughlane.ie; Tue–Thu 9.45am–6pm, Fri–Sat 10am–5pm, Sun 11am–5pm; free) houses modern and contemporary European and Irish artworks. Sir Hugh Lane (1875–1915) established Dublin's Municipal Gallery of Modern Art on Harcourt Street in 1908; the collection was moved here in 1933. There are some 2,000 works by artists such as Manet, Monet, Toulouse Lautrec and the 20th-century Irish painter (and brother of W.B. Yeats) Jack B. Yeats. Since 2001 the museum has also been home to Francis Bacon's studio, reconstructed in its chaotic entirety. There is a café here that makes a pleasant stop for morning coffee.

O'CONNELL STREET

Retrace your steps, and turn right onto Parnell Square East. At the point at which Parnell Square East becomes Upper O'Connell Street stands the **Parnell Monument** ❹, designed by the American sculptor Augustus Saint-Gaudens and erected in 1903–7. The politician Charles Stewart Parnell (1846–91) became a national hero through his campaigns for Irish Home Rule. However in 1886, on being implicated in the divorce case of a married woman, Kitty O'Shea, he suffered a dramatic fall from grace. Parnell's legacy was famously debated in James Joyce's *A Portrait of the Artist as a Young Man* (1916) and *Dubliners* (1914).

Continuing south along O'Connell Street, the **Spire of Dublin** ❺ rises up as if from below ground. With the official title 'Monument of Light', the Spire was the winning entry in a 2002 architectural competition to provide a replacement for Nelson's Column, which was blown up on the site in 1966 by an IRA bomb. It is 120 metres (400ft) in height, and 3 metres (9ft) in diameter at the base, but only 15cm (6in) at the top. Nearby, on the corner with Earl Street North, is a fanciful statue of Joyce.

General Post Office

The Palladian-style **General Post Office** ❻, built in 1818, faces the spire on the western side of O'Connell Street. The GPO was the site of the reading of the 'Proclamation of the Irish Republic' on Easter Monday 1916. The bullet holes on its columns are a reminder of the bloody legacy of that day. Inside, there is a permanent exhibition space dedicated to the Easter Rising (www.gpowitnesshistory.ie; Mon–Fri 9am–5.30pm, Sat–Sun 10am–5.30pm). Almost opposite the GPO is the historic Clerys department store, which is currently under redevelopment.

Daniel O'Connell monument

Continue south down O'Connell Street and the last statue that you pass is the

Wolfe Tone memorial, St Stephen's Green

Daniel O'Connell monument ❼. Known as the 'Liberator', O'Connell (1775–1847) campaigned for Catholic emancipation – the right for Catholics to sit at parliament in Westminster – and for the dissolution of the Act of Union between Ireland and Great Britain.

Crossing the elegant **O'Connell Bridge**, built in the 1790s, will take you over the River Liffey.

GRAFTON STREET AND ST STEPHEN'S GREEN

Continuing south along Westmoreland Street, you will pass the imposing **Bank of Ireland** on your right and the grand entrance to **Trinity College** on your left. Crossing Nassau Street will take you to pedestrianised **Grafton Street**. This area is home to Dublin's most upmarket shops and shopping arcades, like the **Powerscourt Townhouse Centre** (59 South William Street; Mon–Fri 10am–6pm, Thu until 8pm, Sat 9am–6pm, Sun noon–6pm).

Bewley's Oriental Café

About 100 metres/yds down Grafton Street, on your right, is **Bewley's Oriental Café**, currently closed for renovation, see ❶. Dating from 1827, this Dublin institution is crammed full of teas, buns and Art Deco splendour. **Bewley's Café Theatre** (www.bewleyscafetheatre.com; temporarily based in the Powerscourt Townhouse Centre while renovations are completed), with performances at 12.50pm every day except Sunday, is highly recommended. Short plays by the likes of Oscar Wilde and Sean O'Casey, or new Irish writers, are performed as you tuck into a light lunch. Be sure to check out the majestic Harry Clarke stained-glass windows, dating from 1928.

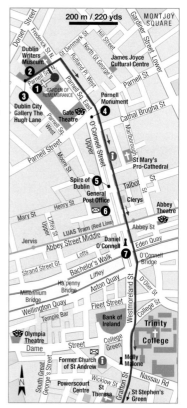

St Stephen's Green   *Robert Emmet, St Stephen's Green*

St Stephen's Green

After lunch, a short stroll south down bustling Grafton Street takes you to leafy **St Stephen's Green** ❽. At the end of Grafton Street, cross over the road and through the Dublin Fusiliers Arch (1904) to enter the green, which was laid out in 1880. Walking around the green in an anti-clockwise direction, you will see statues of Irish patriot Robert Emmet; writers Yeats and Joyce; the Three Fates; and Wolfe Tone, leader of the 1798 Wexford Rebellion. Behind the monument is a memorial to those who died in the Great Famine of 1845–9.

On a sunny day, picnic provisions can be bought from the refurbished **Dunnes** Stores food hall in the basement of the Stephen's Green Shopping Centre.

MERRION ROW AND MERRION SQUARE

Leaving St Stephen's Green by the northeastern gate, turn right to find **Merrion Row**, packed full of trendy cafés and bistros, including **Etto**, see ❷, and **Hugo's**, see ❸.

On the left-hand side is a surprising site: the tiny **Huguenot cemetery** ❾, built in 1693. Tucked in next to the imposing Sherbourne Hotel, the cemetery is usually locked, but you can peer through the railings to see the gravestones of the descendants of the Huguenots, French Protestants who had fled persecution in France. A list of the 239 surnames of those who are buried here can be seen on the wall plaque to the left; this mentions the Becquett family, ancestors of the playwright Samuel Beckett.

Upper Merrion Street

At the end of Merrion Row, turn left onto Upper Merrion Street, home to **Restaurant Patrick Guilbaud**, see ❹, Dublin's most exclusive restaurant. Continuing along Upper Merrion Street, you will see the imposing **Government Buildings** ❿, housing the office of the Prime Minister (Taoiseach), on your left (www.heritageireland.ie; guided tours only,

Easter Rising

On Easter Monday (24 April) 1916, a motley group of armed nationalists seized control of buildings throughout Dublin. Standing on the steps of the GPO, the poet and playwright Padraig Pearse read out the 'Proclamation of the Irish Republic'. A bloody stand-off ensued between British troops and nationalist insurgents, which lasted six days and left a lot of the city centre in ruins. In a much-criticised attempt to halt the insurgents' efforts, the British government arrested 3,430 men and 79 women, and executed 15 of the leaders, including Pearse. This action did much to inspire Irish nationalist feeling, and resentment: as W.B. Yeats put it in his poem 'Easter 1916', 'A terrible beauty is born'.

Georgian doorways, Merrion Square

Sat 10.30am–1.30pm, every hour; free; tickets can be collected on the morning of the tour from the National Gallery). Built in 1911 as the Royal College of Science, the Irish government occupied the northern wing in 1922. The Cabinet Room and the Ceremonial Staircase can be viewed on the tour.

The next building that you will see on your left is the **National Museum of Ireland – Natural History** (www.museum. ie/Natural-History; Tue–Sat 10am–5pm, Sun 2–5pm; free; built in 1856.

Merrion Square

Upper Merrion Street takes you straight to **Merrion Square ⑪**, the most famous of Dublin's Georgian squares, laid out between 1762 and 1764. If you're short of time, you can walk straight up Merrion Square West. However, it is worth taking the time to walk anti-clockwise around the streets that line the square. Beginning at Merrion Square South, the houses progress in descending numerical order: look out for the old residences of W.B. Yeats (nos 82 and 52), the playwright Sheridan le Fanu (no. 70) and Daniel O'Connell (no. 52).

For a glimpse of what life was like in Georgian times you can visit **29 Lower Fitzwilliam Street ⑫** at the southeastern corner of the square (www.esb.ie/no29; closed for renovation until 2020). The house has been restored with period furnishings that reflect the lifestyle of a middle-class family in the late 18th century.

Oscar Wilde House (closed to the public), on the northwestern corner at no. 1, was the first building to be built here. Wilde, born in 1855, lived here for the first 23 years of his life. Just opposite the house on the corner of the park is the whimsical Oscar Wilde Memorial Sculpture by Danny Osbourne, erected in 1997.

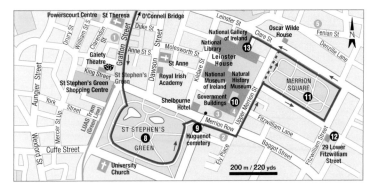

Oscar Wilde statue　　　　　*National Gallery of Ireland*

National Gallery of Ireland

Cross Merrion Square West into Clare Street. Here, on the left, is the entrance to the **National Gallery of Ireland ⑬** (Merrion Square West; www.nationalgallery.ie; Mon–Sat 9.15am–5.30pm, Thu until 8.30pm, Sun 11am–5.30pm; free). First opened in 1864, the gallery houses an enormous collection of Western European art ranging from the Middle Ages to the 20th century. It houses one of the most important collections of Irish art in the world, including the Yeats Museum (named after Jack B. Yeats) and the Millennium Wing, dedicated to modern art.

For a well-earned drink, retrace your steps along Clare Street and turn left into the continuation of Merrion Square West. A right turn onto Fenian Street takes you to watering hole **The Ginger Man**, see ⑤, popular with a young studenty crowd.

Food and Drink

① BEWLEY'S ORIENTAL CAFÉ

78–9 Grafton Street; tel: 01-672 7720; http://bewleys.com; reopening towards the end of 2017 following renovation; €
This cavernous building contains a café bar and deli for breakfast, pastas and pizzas, plus a 'James Joyce' balcony and terrace, which is a favourite spot for afternoon tea (the scones are fabulous). Licensed.

② ETTO

18 Merrion Row; tel: 01-678 8872; www.etto.ie; Mon–Fri noon–10pm, Sat 12.30–10pm; €€
This tiny restaurant offers antipasti and Italian dishes cooked to perfection at reasonable prices. Particularly popular is 'the worker's lunch' for €10. Award-winning casual dining.

③ HUGO'S RESTAURANT AND WINE BAR

6 Merrion Row; tel: 01-676 5955; www.hugos.ie; Sun–Thu noon–10pm, Fri until 11pm, Sat 5–10pm; €€€
An award-winning bar and restaurant, Hugo's offers modern European and fusion cuisine – such as crispy duck confit, seared scallops and wild venison – with an emphasis on locally sourced and organic produce. For a less pricey option, try their pre-theatre menu.

④ RESTAURANT PATRICK GUILBAUD

21 Upper Merrion Street; tel 01-676 4192; www.restaurantpatrickguilbaud.ie; Tue–Sat 12.30–2.15pm, 7–10.15pm; €€€€
With two Michelin stars and a reputation for using the finest seasonal ingredients, this is contemporary French cooking at its best. Avoid bankruptcy with the good-value set lunch.

⑤ THE GINGER MAN

40 Fenian Street; tel: 01-676 6388; daily, until 2.30am at weekends; €€
This traditional Irish pub, set over three floors and with an outdoor terrace, is tucked away behind the Davenport Hotel. There is a good range of beers on tap, the wine is moderately priced, and it serves Irish pub-grub.

Powerscourt Estate

WICKLOW

Wicklow, just south of Dublin, is a county of contrasts, where desolate mountaintop roads give way to plunging river valleys. This route takes in the spectacular scenery of the Great Sugar Loaf Mountain and the Sally Gap, descends into ethereal Glendalough and finishes at the sleepy village of Avoca.

DISTANCE: 75km (47 miles)
TIME: A full day
START: Enniskerry
END: Avoca (or Arklow)
POINTS TO NOTE: Enniskerry is on the R117, 6km (4 miles) south of junction 14 of the M50. If driving from Dublin, the R117 starts south of St Stephen's Green, on Charlemont Street. To return to Dublin at the end of the route, take the R747 from Avoca to Arklow, and then the N11 north. Alternatively, to get to Kilkenny (route 4), travel west on the R747 and R727 to Carlow, and join the N9 and N10 southwest to Kilkenny. As this is a scenic mountain route, with an hour or so between some of the stops, it is worth taking provisions with you. Several points in the route, such as Glencree and Glendalough, offer excellent walking.

This route showcases both the spectacular greenery that has earned Wicklow the title 'garden of Ireland' and the rugged charms of the granite Wicklow Mountains.

It also takes in the Georgian grandeur of the Powerscourt Estate and the mystical delights of Glendalough, one of the oldest monastic settlements in Ireland.

ENNISKERRY AND POWERSCOURT

Begin the route at **Enniskerry ❶**, a quiet country town built into a hillside, where you can buy provisions for the day and have morning coffee and cake at the delightful **Kingfisher's Kitchen**, see ❶, overlooking the town square (note that there is a free car park off the R117, to the west of the square).

Powerscourt Estate and Waterfall
Enniskerry is dominated by the enormous **Powerscourt Estate ❷** (www.powerscourt.ie; daily 9.30am–5.30pm, until dusk in winter), just south of the town. To get there, follow the main road uphill, passing the town square on your right; Powerscourt is clearly signposted off the road. Although the estate dates back to 1300, when the Le Poer family – later anglicised to Power – built a castle

Powerscourt facade

Powerscourt waterfall

here, the Palladian-style mansion and landscaped gardens that you see today were completed in the late 18th century and were restored, following a fire, in the mid-1990s. A visit to the estate gives an insight into the lifestyle of the super-rich Anglo-Irish during the Romantic period.

There is a separate entrance (and entry charge) for the stunning **Powerscourt Waterfall ❸** (daily Mar–Oct 10.30am–5.30pm, Nov–Feb 10.30am–4pm, May–Aug 9.30am–7pm), the highest in Ireland at 121 metres (398ft). To reach it, leave the mansion and gardens and turn right uphill; the road twists and turns for several kilometres.

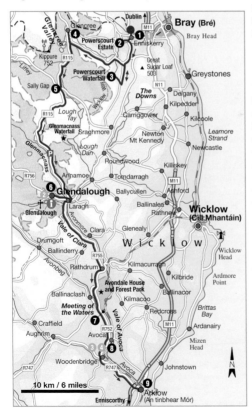

WICKLOW MOUNTAIN DRIVE

Glencree and Sugar Loaf Mountain

Heading back towards the estate, turn left and take the road that skirts the river valley. After about 15 minutes, the road meets the R115. A right turn will take you to the small village of **Glencree ❹**, set into the Glencree valley, with its unusual Peace and Reconciliation Centre (founded in 1974 during 'The Troubles'), former British army barracks and café (see www.glencree.ie).

Glencree affords stunning views, looking east, of the **Great Sugar Loaf Mountain**, Wicklow's highest point at 503 metres (1,650ft).

Glendalough lower-lake scenery

Sally Gap

Leaving Glencree, return to the R115 and follow the road south towards the **Sally Gap ❺**. This desolate, barren mountain pass is surprisingly flat, allowing for astonishing views of the steely Wicklow mountains. There is a parking spot 10km (6 miles) further on at **Glenmacnass**, where you can visit a gorgeous waterfall.

GLENDALOUGH TO AVOCA

The road descends to arrive, after another 10–15 minutes, at the river valley of **Glendalough ❻**. At the end of the R115, take a right along the R756 to reach the free Visitor Centre car park (there is a charge for the higher car park) and the **Visitor Centre** itself (mid-Oct–mid-Mar 9.30am–5pm, mid-Mar–mid-Apr until 6pm).

Avondale House

Just outside Rathdrum, on the L2149, are Avondale House and Forest Park (house: Apr–Sept Thu–Sun 11am–5pm, by appointment rest of year; park: daily 8.30am–5pm; free), the birthplace and home of national hero and later disgraced politician Charles Stewart Parnell. The house, built by James Wyatt in 1779 and surrounded by 202ha (500 acres) of tree trails and walks, was recently restored according to its 1850 decor.

The name Glendalough derives from Irish Gaelic 'Gleann dá Locha', meaning 'Glen of the two Lakes'; the upper lake, a short walk along the river valley, is much the bigger of the two. St Kevin first established a monastic settlement in 498AD, and monks continued to study and live here until the 1600s. The upper lake has the better scenery and the original sites of St Kevin's settlement and habitations. The lower lake contains many impressive architectural sights, including the monastery gatehouse (the only surviving example of its kind in the country), the 10th-century St Mary's Church and tiny round tower, and a 12th-century Priest's House.

Leaving Glendalough, a good option for lunch is the **Wicklow Heather Restaurant**, see ❷.

Vale of Clara

Head back along the R756, following the signs to Avoca. After a few kilometres turn right onto the R755 and continue southeast, driving parallel to the Avonmore River. The road descends into the gently wooded **Vale of Clara**, passing through the small village of **Rathdrum**. Nearby are **Avondale House and Forest Park** (see box).

Meeting of the Waters

Some 8km (5 miles) past Rathdrum (taking the R752 south) is the **Meeting of the Waters ❼**, the point at which the rivers Avonbeg and Avonmore converge to form the River Avoca. Set deep in the

Avoca Handweavers   *Monastery gatehouse, Glendalough*

Vale of Avoca, this is a surprisingly moody place, blanketed by trees. Thomas Moore gave the spot its name in an 1808 poem, which is inscribed on a wall.

Avoca

A few minutes further on, set just off the main road alongside the river, is delightful **Avoca** ❽. Once the location for the 1990s BBC series *Ballykissangel*, the main draw of the village is now **Avoca Handweavers** (Old Mill, Main Street; www.avoca.ie; summer 9am–6pm, winter 9.30am–5.30pm). The weavers here have been producing linens from Ireland's oldest working mill since 1723; you can see them in action in the weaving sheds. The fruits of their labours – including rugs and bed linen, clothing and accessories – are sold here in the mill shop, and in stores throughout Ireland. The mill also has an excellent **café**, see ❸. For fish and chips, **Hendley's**, opposite Fitzgerald's pub, is a good option – see ❹.

Arklow

Continue southeast from Avoca along the R747 to **Arklow** ❾, Wicklow's busiest town and once a thriving port.

Food and Drink

❶ **KINGFISHER'S KITCHEN**
The Square, Enniskerry; tel: 01-276 4859; daily 8.30–5pm; €
Kingfisher's serves freshly made sandwiches, home-made cakes and hot drinks to eat in or take away. There's outdoor seating only (overlooking the main square), but Avoca blankets and cushions are provided.

❷ **WICKLOW HEATHER RESTAURANT**
R756 just before Glendalough (south side of road); tel: 0404-45157; www.wicklow heather.ie; Mon–Thu 8am–9.30pm, Fri–Sat until 10pm, Sun until 9pm; €€
A pub/restaurant on the tourist trail with prices to match. The menu is much better value at lunch, when you can get a goat's cheese open sandwich or a crispy chicken salad, as well as

mains and specials. You can enjoy your meal on the pleasant outdoor terrace.

❸ **AVOCA HANDWEAVERS CAFÉ AND STORE**
The Mill at Avoca Village; tel: 0402-35105; www.avoca.ie; daily 9am–6pm (winter 9.30am–5.30pm); €
Inside the Avoca Handweavers is a retro-style café and deli, selling delicious tea, cakes, soup and sandwiches.

❹ **HENDLEY'S FISH AND CHIP RESTAURANT AND TAKEAWAY**
Avoca Village; tel: 0402-30937; Wed–Sun noon–1pm; €
More than your average fish-and-chip restaurant, Hendley's serves the 'daily catch' as well as smoked fish specials at very reasonable prices. Right on the river.

Kilkenny Castle

KILKENNY

Explore Kilkenny's castle and medieval centre before driving through picturesque villages on the River Nore to tranquil Jerpoint Abbey deep in the countryside. Finish off aboard a famine ship at New Ross in County Wexford.

DISTANCE: City walk: 2km (1.25 miles); drive: 46km (28.5 miles)
TIME: A 2-hour city walk followed by a half-day drive
START: Kilkenny city
END: New Ross
POINTS TO NOTE: Kilkenny is 116km (72 miles) southwest of Dublin and approximately 100km (62 miles) west of Arklow. New Ross is 14km (8 miles) northeast of Waterford, starting point of route 5, and 53km (33 miles) west of Rosslare ferry terminal.

KILKENNY CITY

Kilkenny ❶ was founded by St Canice in the 6th century; in its 14th-century heyday it was the venue for many English parliaments, rivalling Dublin in importance. Its compact centre has several medieval buildings and cobbled alleyways off the main street known as 'slips', but the star of the show is Kilkenny Castle, set in rich parklands beside the River Nore.

Kilkenny Castle

Follow signs for the city centre which will lead you to **Kilkenny Castle ❶** (www.kilkennycastle.ie, daily Oct–Feb 9.30am–4.30pm, Mar, Sept until 5pm, Apr–May until 5.30pm, June–Aug 9am–5.30pm), an unmistakable landmark beside a large public car park. The original castle was built in the 13th century, but the present building dates mainly from 1820. Inside its huge entrance gate you are greeted by a magnificent panorama in which the mature trees of the castle's parklands frame the distant countryside, with a formal rose garden and fountain in the foreground. The seat of the Butler family (the Dukes of Ormond), two wings of the castle have been restored in the style of a grand country house circa 1830. They contain a library, drawing room and long gallery.

Kilkenny Design Craft Centre

Cross the road in front of the castle to visit its stable block, an elegant semi-circular construction in the classical style, topped by a copper dome and weather vane. It now houses the **Kilkenny Design Craft**

Centre ❶ (www.kilkennydesign.com; Mon–Sat 10am–7pm), one of Ireland's best craft shops. Also here is the headquarters of the Crafts Council of Ireland, which has exhibitions of contemporary craft work (free), and a restaurant. There are also several small craft studios and factory outlets. A gate at the rear leads to the pleasant gardens of **Butler House** (www.butler.ie), the castle's dower house.

Medieval town centre

Turn left out of the Design Centre, past some fine 18th-century houses, and turn right at the traffic lights onto Rose Inn Street. **Shee Alms House** ❸, a stone building constructed in 1594 to house the poor, is now the **Tourist Information Office** (www.kilkennytourism. ie). Go up to the first floor, and exit onto a narrow alleyway, turning left. This leads to the High Street.

Turn right and walk past the **Tholsel** ❹, Kilkenny's former toll-house, which was built in 1761 and has an arcade over the pavement and an octagonal clock tower. Beyond this, on the opposite side of the road, is **Rothe House and Garden** ❺ (Parliament Street; www. rothehouse.com; Mon– Sat 10.30am–5pm, Sun noon–5pm), a 16th-century merchant's fortified home, which now houses a museum of local history.

St Canice's Cathedral

From Rothe House, on your left you can see **St Canice's Cathedral** ❻ (www.stcanicescathedral. ie; Mon–Sat 10am–1pm, 2–5pm, Sun 2–5pm, with exceptions), named after the city's founder, on a height above the town. It is approached from Parliament Street up a flight of stone steps and under an arch. The cathedral, with its massive round tower and stepped bat-

200 m / 220 yds

The Tholsel

tlements, dates from the 13th century, and is believed to be on the site of St Canice's monastic foundation. Oliver Cromwell's soldiers left it a roofless ruin, and it has been much restored over the years, but it still has some fine medieval monuments. Wooden steps inside the 30-metre (98ft) tall **round tower** can be climbed (no children under 12).

Black Abbey

Leave the cathedral by the main gate leading to Dean Street. Cross over and follow the finger signpost down an alley that crosses a canal to the **Dominican Church**. It incorporates the slender tower and 14th-century windows of the **Black Abbey** ⑤, dating from 1225; in the forecourt is an unusual collection of mid-13th-century stone coffins.

Turn left out of the church and follow the 'slip' back to Parliament Street. Turn right, and at the fork take the lower street, St Kieran's, a lively pedestrianised area, once the heart of the medieval town; it leads back to Rose Inn Street and the castle.

NORE VALLEY

Head straight out of town from the castle and join the R700, a pretty minor road that follows the River Nore southwards to its estuary.

Bennettsbridge

The stone bridge at **Bennettsbridge** ②, 6km (3.75 miles) south of Kilkenny, dates from 1285 and is one of the oldest crossings of the River Nore. The road swings right over the bridge, and passes **Nicholas Mosse Pottery** (www.nicholas mosse.com), which sells handmade pottery and marks the start of the **Kilkenny Craft Trail** (www.kilkennytourism.ie/craft_trail) of local craft outlets.

Thomastown and Jerpoint Abbey

Thomastown ③, 12km (7 miles) further south, is an attractive village of

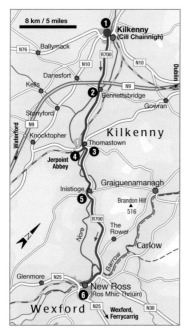

St Canice's Cathedral   *Jerpoint Abbey*

grey-stone buildings and steep hills that dates from the 13th century. You could stop for lunch here at the **Watergarden Café**, see ①.

Follow the signs in the village for a 2km (1 mile) detour southwest across another narrow stone bridge to **Jerpoint Abbey** ❹ (www.heritageireland. ie; daily Mar–Oct 9am–5pm, Nov–early Dec 9.30am–4pm). Founded in 1158 by the Cistercians, this is one of the finest monastic ruins in Ireland, consisting of a cloister, quadrangle and three-naved church with Romanesque arches set against a peaceful rural backdrop. Walk around the two sides of the cloisters to appreciate their unusual carvings, some of which are like medieval cartoons.

Inistioge

Return to Thomastown and re-join the R700 south, crossing the Nore again via a long, 12-arched stone bridge, amid sweeping views of a wooded valley, the location of **Inistioge** ❺. The village is situated on a bend of the river and has a tree-lined square leading to a tall stone bridge. It's a favourite location for films, which include *Widow's Peak* (1994) with Mia Farrow and Joan Plowright, *Circle of Friends* (1995) with Minnie Driver and Saffron Burrows, and *The Secret Scripture* (2016). Follow the road to the left at the Woodstock Arms for the riverfront. A flat grassy area next to the river is a perfect spot for picnicking, with a view of the picturesque bridge backed by a line of Georgian houses.

NEW ROSS

Continue along the R700 for another 17km (10.5 miles), crossing the border into County Wexford at **New Ross** ❻. The town was built on a steep hill overlooking the River Barrow at a strategically important river crossing. On the river bank you will see the tall masts of the ***Dunbrody Famine Ship*** (www.dunbrody.com; tours daily 9am–6pm), a full-scale replica of a sailing ship built in 1845 to transport emigrants to North America. On board, actors tell the stories of the passengers, who travelled in appalling conditions in this 'coffin-ship' in order to escape the Great Famine. It is both an entertaining and sobering reminder of the ordeal suffered by the 2 million plus people who emigrated from this port.

Food and Drink

① WATERGARDEN CAFÉ

Ladywell Street, Thomastown; tel: 056-772 4690; Tue–Fri 10am–4pm; €

This simple café, beside a garden centre and craft shop, backs onto a delightful stream-side garden overhung by weeping willows. Enjoy a delicious light lunch of soup, salad and desserts.

Waterford Crystal factory tour

WATERFORD AND THE ROCK OF CASHEL

Explore Waterford city's 18th-century quayside then drive to the iconic Rock of Cashel. Cross the scenic Vee Gap through the Knockmealdown Mountains then potter around pretty Lismore village, dominated by a grey-stone castle.

DISTANCE: 122km (76 miles)
TIME: A full day
START: Waterford city
END: Lismore
POINTS TO NOTE: On Sundays, some sights and more individual shops in Waterford city may be closed. From Waterford to Cashel via Clonmel is 71km (44 miles). If you are driving to the southwest from Dublin, start the route at Cashel. From Cashel to Lismore is 51km (32 miles). From Lismore you can return to Waterford (63km/39 miles) on the N72 and N25 or continue west on the N72 to Fermoy and N8 to Cork (49.5km/30 miles).

Waterford is the largest city in the southeast, but even then it only has a population of about 50,000. Founded by the Vikings in 853, it was the first settlement to be occupied by the Normans, who came from Wales in 1170. It owes its historic importance to its sheltered location on the mouth of the River Suir, and its proximity to the Welsh coast.

The rural counties of Waterford and Tipperary have rich fertile plains and small, quiet towns. The mighty Rock of Cashel, once home to the Kings of Munster, is a legacy of the area's wealth and strategic importance in pre-Christian and medieval times.

WATERFORD CITY

In its 18th-century heyday **Waterford** ❶ was an important port, and its long quays, though awaiting redevelopment, are still impressive. Quaint, cobbled streets alternate with gracefully proportioned Georgian buildings. The building of the largely pedestrianised shopping centre unearthed many treasures from its Viking and Norman past, now displayed in a fine museum.

The quays

Park on the quays, and if the weather is fine, stroll up towards the town clock along the once busy cut-stone docks. Then head for the unmistakable

Waterford Crystal chandeliers

pepper-pot bastion **Reginald's Tower** (www.heritageireland.ie; Apr–mid-Dec daily 9.30am–5.30pm, Jan–Mar Wed–Sun until 5pm) at the quays' eastern extremity. This 12th-century drum tower is 24 metres (80ft) tall and has been used as a mint, prison and military store. It is now restored and houses a collection of treasures that includes Viking and Norman artefacts unearthed in recent excavations. Highlights include a gold brooch from 1210AD, a sword given by Henry VIII to Waterford's Mayor in 1536, and 18th-century Irish silver. The ground floor is home to one of the town's most popular daytime eating spots, **The Granary**, see ①.

Waterford Crystal Visitor Centre

Turn right out of Reginald's Tower and walk inland along the Mall to the headquarters of **Waterford Crystal** (www.waterfordvisitorcentre.com; factory tours Nov–Feb Mon–Fri 9am–3.15pm, Mar–Oct Mon–Sat until 4.15pm, Sun 9.30am–4.15pm). 'Old Waterford Glass', a heavy lead crystal produced between 1783 and 1851, is much sought-after by collectors for its outstanding light-refracting properties. Following bankruptcy in 2009, Waterford Crystal is again being produced in the city, and the dramatic factory tour is as popular as ever. Book in advance online to avoid queuing.

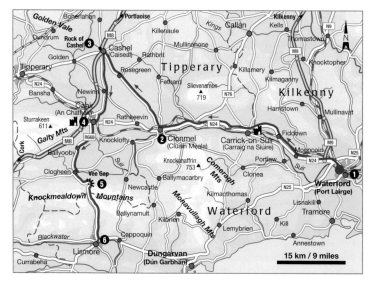

Rock of Cashel

ROCK OF CASHEL

Leave Waterford on the N24, heading west through **Carrick-on-Suir** and **Clonmel ❷**. The latter is a busy market town on the River Suir known for its apple orchards and cider-making. About 500 metres/yds west of Clonmel, take the R688 northwest to Cashel.

The **Rock of Cashel ❸** (www.heritageireland.ie; daily 9am–5.30pm, June–mid-Sept until 7pm, mid-Oct–mid-Mar until 4.30pm), a 63-metre (206ft) limestone outcrop topped with ruined towers and gables, looms up suddenly from the flat plain. Its unexpected beauty causes a sharp intake of breath.

The Rock was originally a stronghold of the Kings of Munster who ruled southwest Ireland during the early Middle Ages. On converting to Christianity in 1101, King Muirchertach Ua Briain gave his fortress to the Church. Most of the buildings here date from the 13th to 15th centuries.

Exploring the Rock

After buying your ticket, turn right into the enclosure to avoid following the herd, then stroll around the northern perimeter, enjoying views of the plains of Tipperary. Note the high-up entrance at the base of the round tower, which made it a safe refuge.

Now walk through the roofless Gothic cathedral to the **Crossing**, a complex arch where two churches interlink. Turn left out of the cathedral to **Cormac's Chapel** (access by guided tour only from May–Sept each year due to restoration work), one of Europe's finest examples of Hiberno-Romanesque architecture. Look up at the huge rounded arches above each of the doors, and the ingenious curved roof.

Cashel town

It is only a few minutes' walk south, past an old chapel now converted into a fine-dining restaurant, **Chez Hans**, and an adjacent daytime café, to the centre of **Cashel**, a quiet country town with some old-fashioned wooden shop fronts. Turn south for the **Heritage Centre** (Main Street; www.cashel.ie; daily 9.30am–5.30pm, with exceptions in winter; free), which has a display about the historical relationship between the town and the Rock, and a scale model of Cashel in the 1600s; it also contains the Tourist Information Office.

VEE GAP

Drive south on the N8, taking the R670 for **Cahir ❹** and following it as it turns sharply right down a hill through the town. Cahir's most notable feature is its **castle** (www.heritageireland.ie; daily 9.30am–5.30pm, mid-Oct–Feb until 4.30pm), a massive 12th-century limestone fortress set on a rock in the River Suir.

The R668 to Clogheen is on the left immediately after the castle. As you

Tipperary from Vee Gap

Lismore Castle

drive towards Ballylooby, the **Knockmealdown Mountains** are straight ahead. Take a sharp left in **Clogheen** for the **Vee Gap ⑤**, a scenic mountain pass. The road curves around a peat-covered mountain, past a black corrie lake, to a height of 653 metres (2,144ft). Park here and look back across the flat plain of Tipperary to Cahir at the foot of the Galtee Mountains. Up here, there are no inhabitants (just sheep) and the vegetation is mainly grass and heather. Descending into the valley of the Blackwater River, the vegetation increases, with rhododendrons and a rich undergrowth of ferns.

LISMORE

Continue south on the R688. As you cross the bridge into **Lismore ⑥** you will have a dramatic view of **Lismore Castle**, perched on a cliff above the River Blackwater. This mid-19th-century building is the Irish residence of the Duke of Devonshire; it is not open to the public. The village itself was home to a 6th-century monastery founded by St Carthage and was built to house the workers on the Duke's estates; during the famine years the people of Lismore suffered particularly badly.

Park and walk to the **Lismore Heritage Centre** (www.discoverlismore.com; Mon–Fri 9am–5.30pm, Apr–Oct also Sat 10am–5.30pm and Sun noon–5.30pm). Formerly the town courthouse, the centre has a shop, tourist information, and a video presentation on the town's history.

Village walk

Turn right and walk along Lismore's main street. Among the pleasant mix of shops and antiques stores are several pubs and restaurants. Turn left up the broad North Mall, which leads to **St Carthage's Cathedral** (daily 9.30am–5.30pm; free), a modest mid-17th-century church in the neo-Gothic style with some interesting memorial stones from an earlier 9th-century church. Take the cobbled footpath to the left of the church leading downhill, and turn left at the main road to return to the car park.

Just here is the entrance to **Lismore Castle Gardens and Art Gallery** (www.lismorecastle.com; daily Apr–Sept 10.30am–5.30pm). The 3ha (7 acres) of gardens consist of woodland walks and contemporary sculpture, with good views of the castle.

Food and Drink

❶ THE GRANARY

Hanover Street, Merchant's Quay, Waterford; tel: 051-854 428; www.granary cafe.ie; Mon–Sat 8am–5pm; €
The self-service counter is packed with home-baked treats like lemon meringue pie or foccacia. There's a sheltered outdoor patio, and sofas and tables in the museum lobby.

River view

CORK CITY AND HARBOUR

After a walking tour of the centre of Cork city, including its bustling indoor food market and renowned art gallery, visit a thriving wildlife park, a classic shooting lodge surrounded by gardens and Cobh, formerly Queenstown, departure point for most of Ireland's 19th- and 20th-century emigrants.

DISTANCE: City walk: 0.75km (0.5 miles); drive: 24.5km (15 miles)
TIME: 1 or 2 days
START: Cork city
END: Cobh
POINTS TO NOTE: Allow two days if you include a visit to the university. Note that Cork is busiest on Saturdays and quietest on Mondays. Many city attractions are closed on Sundays. Trains run to Fota and Cobh every half hour from Kent Station (Lower Glanmire Road; 021-455 7277; www.irishrail.ie), on the city's northern side. From Cork, you can head 30km (18 miles) south to Kinsale (route 7), or west on the N22 to Killarney and the Ring of Kerry (route 8) and Tralee and the Dingle Peninsula (route 9).

Cork's city centre is built on an island formed by two channels of the River Lee. In the 18th and early 19th century cargoes of butter, beef and animal hides were exported from the city's many quays, creating a rich merchant class who built an attractive city of bridges and steeples. In the 19th century shipping moved downstream to the deep-water harbour at Cobh. The view of Cobh's steeply terraced houses beneath the soaring Gothic cathedral was the last, often tear-blurred, sight most emigrants had of their homeland.

The northern side of the city rises steeply from the river and wits like to joke that this is the origin of the distinctly 'up and down' Cork accent. You will hear fine examples of this on St Patrick Street in the afternoons, when newspaper sellers hawk the *Evening Echo* with loud cries of 'Eeeeeko'.

CORK CITY

Start at the **Tourist Information Office** (www.discoverireland.ie; Mon–Sat 9am–5pm) on **Grand Parade ❶**. Directly across the road note the terrace of three elegant Georgian houses with slate-hung, bow-fronted windows, remnants of Cork's 18th-century prime.

English Market

English Market

Turn right for the **English Market** ❷ (www.englishmarket.ie; Mon–Sat 8am–6pm), a Victorian covered market. Step back to view the imposing classical entrance. (It's worth looking up regularly in Cork to enjoy the ornate Victorian facades that often survive above the modern shop fronts.) A foodie-heaven, the market has about 150 stalls, from traditional butchers to purveyors of farmhouse cheeses and hand-made chocolates – do not miss the alley of freshly landed seafood. Walking straight through the market will bring you to a piazza where **Farmgate Café** occupies an overhead balcony, see ❶.

St Patrick and Paul Streets

Turn left from the market into Princes' Street and then right onto **St Patrick Street** ❸, a wide curved thoroughfare and the traditional place for a Saturday afternoon promenade. Cross the street and follow the pedestrian alley to **Paul Street** ❹. This is Cork's 'left bank', with antiques shops, bookshops, art galleries, boutiques, cafés and buskers.

Crawford Municipal Art Gallery

At the northeastern end of Paul Street, the **Crawford Municipal Art Gallery** ❺ (Emmett Place; www.crawfordartgallery.ie; Mon–Sat 10am–5pm, Thu until 8pm; free) is a large, Dutch-style red-brick building that dates from 1724; it was originally Cork's Custom House. The collection is strong on 18th–21st-century British and Irish painting, stained glass and classical sculpture. There is a café with excellent fresh food.

Turn left from the gallery and walk past the 1965 **Cork Opera House** along a wide piazza. This leads to the River Lee, with the steep northern side of Cork city opposite. Turn right (east) for **St Patrick's Bridge** ❻, the northern extremity

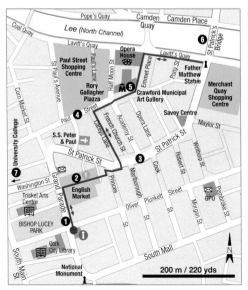

Giraffes at Fota Wildlife Park

of Patrick Street, which you can follow back to Grand Parade.

University College

To extend your city tour, hop on a no. 8 bus outside Debenham's department store on St Patrick Street to **Univer-** **sity College Cork ❼** (Western Road; www.ucc.ie; visitor centre Mon–Fri 9am–5pm, Sat noon–5pm; free), with some 15,000 students. Highlights here include the Tudor-Gothic-style quadrangle (1854), the Crawford Observatory (1878), the Hiberno-Romanesque-style Honan Chapel (1916), the Glucksman Gallery (2005), displaying contemporary art, and a superb collection of Ogham stones inscribed with the Celtic alphabet.

CORK HARBOUR

You can travel to Fota and Cobh either by rail or road. Note that the 25-minute train ride from Kent Station provides dramatic sea views that cannot be seen from a car. If you are driving, you should follow the N8 then the N22 east, turning off at the Fota and Cobh signpost after 10km (6 miles).

Fota Island

Fota Island ❽ and Cobh are both on the shores of Cork's outer harbour. The 47ha (116 acre) estate of Fota House is surrounded by several kilometres of stone wall, and contains a golf course and luxury hotel. Go to the second entrance for **Fota Wildlife Park** (www.fotawildlife.ie; Mon–Sun 10am–4.30pm), which has giraffes, wallabies, ostriches, zebras and antelopes roaming free, plus a large enclosure for cheetahs. The car park also serves **Fota House, Gardens and Arbo-**

Kiss the Blarney

Blarney Castle (www.blarneycastle.ie; daily 9am–6.30pm, Sun until 5.30pm, earlier closing in winter), 10km (6 miles) northwest of Cork city, is still a must for first-time visitors. The building itself (one of Ireland's biggest tower houses) is impressive in bulk, although it is a roofless ruin, and you must climb a spiral of 84 stone steps (wear trainers) to reach the top. To kiss the famous Blarney Stone – in the hope of acquiring 'the gift of the gab' – you need to lie on your back and lean your head out over the castle's ramparts while being held securely by staff who handle some 300,000 stone-kissers a year. The 15th-century castle is situated in a landscaped park with a large lake and two rivers, and is surrounded by 'Druidic' rock gardens. The whole experience is presented tongue-in-cheek as a load of Blarney, but nevertheless makes a good half-day outing. Across the village green at Ireland's biggest craft shop, Blarney Woollen Mills (www.blarney.com), you can acquire a sweater and a woolly hat to complete your Irish initiation.

Colourful Cobh houses

retum (tel: 021-481 5543; www.fota house.com; gardens: daily 9am–6pm; house: Apr–Sept Mon–Sat 10am–5pm, Sun 11am–4pm, Oct–Mar phone ahead). The arboretum is over 200 years old and includes rhododendrons and azaleas (at their best in late spring). The Regency-style house was originally a shooting lodge; its servants' quarters retain many original features and there are impressive plaster ceilings in the ground-floor rooms.

Cobh

The road from Fota to **Cobh** ❾ (pronounced 'cove') skirts the edge of Cork Harbour for 6km (3.75 miles). About 1km (0.5 miles) beyond the cranes of an abandoned dockyard, look out for a signpost on the right to **Cobh Heritage Centre** (www.cobhheritage.com; Mon–Sat 9.30am–6pm, Sun 11am–6pm) and park beside it. If you are coming by train, the station is next to the Heritage Centre.

The Centre occupies a Victorian railway station beside a deep-water berth once used by transatlantic liners. Cobh was the last port of call for the 'unsinkable' RMS *Titanic* in 1912 and also received survivors and the drowned from RMS *Lusitania*, sunk off the coast by a German submarine in 1915. At the time, the town was called Queenstown, having been renamed to celebrate the visit of Queen Victoria in 1849 (it reverted to Cobh in 1920). Within the Centre, **The Queenstown Story** is a lively audiovisual display about the town's seafaring past and Irish emigration.

From here, walk towards the town, an attractive south-facing Victorian resort. The seafront has a Victorian town park and opposite is the **Lusitania Memorial**, dedicated to the 1,198 people who died when the ocean liner sank on 7 May 1915. Overhead is the tall spire of the neo-Gothic **St Colman's Cathedral**. Walk up to its entrance for a fine view of Cork Harbour and its islands, with the open sea beyond.

Food and Drink

❶ FARMGATE CAFÉ

English Market, Princes Street; tel: 021-427 8134; Mon–Sat 8.30am–5pm; €
A unique venue on a terrace above the English Market's bustle. All food is sourced in the market.

Charles Fort

WEST CORK COAST

Spend a day exploring the rural coastline of west County Cork, starting in Kinsale, a historic port turned fashionable resort, then meandering along coastal roads and through quiet countryside to the sheltered waters and lush vegetation of Bantry Bay and Glengarriff.

DISTANCE: 136km (85 miles)
TIME: A full day
START: Charles Fort, Kinsale
END: Glengarriff
POINTS TO NOTE: A car is essential for this route. At the end, either return to Kinsale on the R586 from Bantry (88km/54 miles) or push on 27km (17 miles) to Kenmare, or 80km (50 miles) to Killorglin, on the Ring of Kerry (route 8).

Once a run-down rural backwater, west Cork coast's proximity to Cork Airport, its friendly people and its unspoilt environment have led many to buy holiday homes in the area, while others have relocated permanently, bringing prosperity to the region. This route heads west, skirting rocky headlands.

KINSALE

Charles Fort

Approaching Kinsale from Cork, look out for a signpost to **Charles Fort ❶** (www.heritageireland.ie; daily mid-Mar–Oct 10am–6pm, Nov–mid-Mar until 5pm), 2km (1 mile) outside town on the outer harbour. This massive star-shaped fort encloses 3ha (8 acres) of land and was built in 1680. In clear weather you can see the **Old Head of Kinsale**, the western extremity of the beautiful fjord-like harbour. Drive north along the coast road into town.

Kinsale Town

Kinsale ❷, 29km (18 miles) south of Cork city, overlooks the estuary of the Bandon River. Its narrow streets and tall Georgian houses are clustered around the sides of a conical hill. Before becoming a fashionable resort famous for its restaurants, Kinsale was best known for the Battle of Kinsale (1601), in which the combined forces of the (Catholic) Irish and Spanish armies were defeated by the (Protestant) English. After this rout the Irish clan chiefs left for Europe and never returned.

Park on the quay, walk up Pearse Street and then turn left then right for **Desmond Castle**, a 15th-century tower house, containing the **International Museum of Wine** (Cork Street; www.

Kinsale

heritageireland.ie; Apr–mid-Sept daily 10am–6pm). The museum celebrates the Irish families who took up winemaking after leaving for France in the 17th century; their names may be familiar: Hennessy, Barton, Lynch, Dillon...

Check out Kinsale's reputation for high-quality food by dining at **Bastion**, see ❶.

THE ROAD TO SKIBBEREEN

The R600 crosses the River Bandon heading west to quieter country where a slow pace of life prevails. The road follows a wide sea inlet to **Timoleague** ❸, a sleepy village where the ruins of a 14th-century **Franciscan friary** overlook the estuary.

Drombeg Stone Circle
You will only glimpse **Clonakilty** ❹, a pretty market town with traditional wooden shop fronts and carefully tended floral displays,

as you bypass it on the N71. On the inlet at **Rosscarbery** ❺, flocks of swans glide by. About 200 metres/yds further on, take the R597 west (left) for Glandore. After about 5km (3 miles) a sign leads to **Drombeg Stone Circle** ❻, sited on a plateau facing the distant sea. This is one of the most complete of the region's mysterious early Bronze Age remains. A burial, carbon-dated to 1124–794BC, was excavated at the centre of the ring of 14 stones, but nobody knows who built the circle or what it signified to them. Locally, it is believed to be in alignment with the setting sun at the winter solstice. Beside it is a Bronze Age cooking pit, with full instructions.

Millionaire's Row
Continue west to **Glandore** ❼, a line of south-facing houses perched on top of a cliff, nicknamed 'Millionaire's Row'. There is a magical view over a pair of islands to the open sea beyond. In

Old Head of Kinsale

sunny weather it is hard to resist an outdoor drink; try **Hayes' Bar**, see ❷.

Skibbereen

Follow the narrow road through Glandore along the wooded estuary, re-joining the N71 at **Leap**. Continue west to **Skibbereen** ❽, a small market town, once a major junction on the West Cork Railway. The tiny **Skibbereen Heritage Centre** (Upper Bridge Street; www.skibbheritage.com; mid-May–mid-Sept Mon–Sat 10am–6pm, mid-Sept–Oct and mid-Mar–mid-May Tue–Sat 10am–6pm) explains the Great Famine of 1845–9, which took the lives of more than 100,000 people locally.

As it approaches **Ballydehob** ❾, a brightly painted hill village, the N71 turns inland and climbs across remote, sparsely inhabited hills, some planted with Sitka spruce, before winding down to gentler climes.

If you like lighthouses, detour 22.5km (14 miles) southwest from Ballydehob on the R592 to the **Mizen Head Visitor Centre** (www.mizenhead.net; mid-Mar–Oct daily 10.30am–5/6pm, winter Sat–Sun 11am–4pm only). The centre is in the lighthouse-keeper's house on an island at the tip of the rocky peninsula, accessed by a suspension bridge.

BANTRY BAY

Bantry ❿, a quiet seaport and market town, is at the southeastern corner of the bay of the same name. The rafts that you see on the bay are evidence of the biggest local industry: mussel farming. You can sample the product in town at **O'Connor's Seafood Restaurant**, see ❸.

Bantry House and Garden (www.bantryhouse.com; Apr–May, Sept–Oct Tue–Sun 10am–5pm, June–Aug daily 10am–5pm) is set on a height overlooking the 6.5km (4 mile) wide bay and the serried ranks of surrounding mountains. The large mid-18th-century mansion is well worth a visit. Its interior contains a fine selection of treasures brought back by the first Earl of Bantry from Europe in the early 19th century, and there is an extensive garden.

Glengarriff and Garinish Island

Beyond Bantry, the N71 runs along the water's edge through wooded **Ballylickey**, rising to a height above Bantry Bay, where there are several viewing points. Then it's downhill again to **Glengarriff** ⓫, a sheltered inlet at the top of the bay with a sub-tropical climate. The

Lighthouse at the Old Head of Kinsale

Bantry House

harbour here is presided over by the **Glengarriff Eccles Hotel**, see ❹.

Continue into the village and park near Quills Woollen Market. Beside the public toilets is a kiosk selling tickets for **boat trips** from the Blue Pool ferry point. Choose between an hour-long **harbour trip**, with close-up views of basking seals, or a visit to **Garinish Island** (also known as Illnacullin; www.garnishisland.com; May–Sept Mon–Sat 10am–6pm, Sun noon–6pm, Oct Mon–Sat 10am–4pm, Sun 1–5pm, Apr Mon–Sat 10am–5.30pm, Sun 1–6pm), 10 minutes offshore. In the early 20th century the 15ha (37 acres) of land on the island were transformed into a series of formal and informal gardens, using unusual shrubs and rare subtropical flowers, the whole framed by the rocky peaks of the surrounding hills.

For a scenic walk, drive through the busy village to **Glengarriff Woods Nature Reserve** (www.glengarriffnaturereserve.ie), where there are a number of way-marked trails.

Food and Drink

❶ BASTION

Junction Market Street and Main Street, Kinsale; tel: 021-470 9696; www.bastionkinsale.com; Wed–Sat 5–11pm; €€€
Foodie heaven in a smartly designed contemporary restaurant. Imaginative spin on traditional dishes, such as bacon and cabbage. Wonderfully attentive service.

❷ HAYES' BAR

The Square, Glandore; tel: 028-33214; daily noon–9pm; €
This simple local has a superb bay view and offers a surprising range of wines by the glass. Local prawns, crab and salmon are served in open sandwiches and West Cork farmhouse cheese features in the croque monsieur.

❸ O'CONNOR'S SEAFOOD RESTAURANT

The Square, Bantry; tel: 027-55664; www.oconnorseafood.com; daily noon–9.30pm; €€€
This superb town centre restaurant offers up a shoal of seafood delights, including chowder, oysters, calamari, fresh lobster by the pound and mussels prepared in three different ways. Meat eaters and vegetarians are also catered for.

❹ GLENGARIFF ECCLES HOTEL RESTAURANT

Glengarriff Harbour; tel: 027-63003; www.eccleshotel.com; daily noon–9pm (hotel closes Oct–mid-Jan); €€
All kinds of notable writers have stayed here, from William Thackeray to W.B. Yeats to Virginia Woolf. The food is standard hotel/bar fare, but you should visit this large 250-year-old hotel for its splendid location overlooking Glengarriff Harbour and the atmosphere of Victorian grandeur that persists.

THE RING OF KERRY

The Ring of Kerry is one of Europe's great scenic drives, a circular route around the rim of the Iveragh Peninsula, through rugged sandstone hills and lush subtropical vegetation, with spectacular mountain and coastal views.

DISTANCE: 140km (87 miles)
TIME: 1 or 2 days
START: Killorglin
END: Kenmare
POINTS TO NOTE: A car is essential to tour the Ring independently. Tour bus traffic leaves Killarney 16km (10 miles) east of Killorglin between 9am and 10am travelling anti-clockwise, so leave earlier or later. If heavy rain is forecast, make other plans. Allow two days if you intend to visit the Skellig Rocks, a 3–4 hour boat trip; book ahead and bear in mind the ferry leaves Portmagee at 10am.

The Ring of Kerry follows the coast of the Iveragh Peninsula in the extreme southwest. The route overlooks Dingle Bay to the north, the open Atlantic to the west and the sheltered waters of Kenmare Bay to the south. Inland, to the east, are the purple hills known as Macgillycuddy's Reeks and the Lakes of Killarney. The Gulf Stream ensures a mild, frost-free climate.

DINGLE BAY

At **Killorglin** ❶ on the River Laune join the Ring of Kerry (N70) by driving west across the river and up the steep main street. This market town is known for its annual Puck Fair, a street festival held in August (see www.puckfair.ie).

Kerry Bog Village Museum

The scenery begins about 8km (5 miles) beyond Killorglin amid wild, sparsely inhabited hills. Stop at the **Red Fox Inn** for the **Kerry Bog Village Museum** ❷ (www.kerrybogvillage.ie; daily 9.30am–6pm), three reconstructed cottages with turf fires, ponies and dogs. It commemorates a simple rural lifestyle which persisted until the mid-20th century.

Rossbeigh

Just beyond tiny **Glenbeigh**, detour 2km (1.25 miles) on the R564 to **Rossbeigh** ❸, a 6.5km (4 mile) sandy beach facing north across Dingle Bay. Take a few minutes to get your bearings and enjoy the sea air. After Glenbeigh the road curves dramatically towards the

Coastal view on the Ring of Kerry

coast, following a cliff top between the mountains and the pounding Atlantic.

Cahirciveen

Cahirciveen ❹ is the chief market town of south Kerry, but usually has a deserted air, even more than 150 years after being devastated by the Famine. Park near the **Tourist Information Office** (Church Street) and walk down the side road to the **Old Barracks** (www.oldbarrackscahersiveen.com; Mon–Fri 10am–4.30pm, Sat 11.30am–4.30pm, Sun 1–5pm), an exotic white turreted building that once housed the local constabulary. Restored as a heritage centre, it has informative displays on local history, including the Famine. From here, you can see the estuary of the Carhen River, the more attractive side of town.

Back at the main road turn west to the **O'Connell Memorial Church**, a huge Gothic-style edifice with a black limestone facade, built in 1888.

ATLANTIC COAST

As you leave Cahirciveen, the **Valentia Observatory**, now part of the Irish meteorological service, is on the right. It was originally sited on Valentia Island in 1868, because the island had a telegraphic link to London and was in the path of most weather systems coming in from the Atlantic.

Portmagee and Skellig Rocks

Shortly beyond the observatory, head west for 12km (7.5 miles) to **Portmagee ❺**, a tiny fishing village and the departure

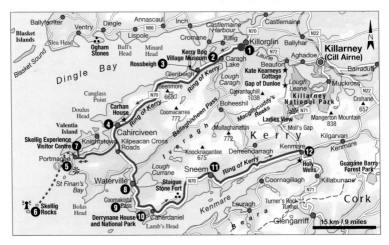

Lough Leane, Killarney

point for the boat trip to Skellig Rocks. Go to where the Stars Wars actors hung out – the final scene of *Star Wars: The Force Awakens* was filmed on Skellig Michael – at **The Bridge Bar**, see ⓘ.

Weather permitting, small open boats make the 13km (8 mile) crossing from Portmagee to **Skellig Rocks** ❻ (leaves 10am; www.skelligexperience.com/other-sea-tours) in about an hour. **Little Skellig** is home to over 27,000 gannets, while **Skellig Michael** (where landing is permitted) rises to a double peak 217 metres (712ft) high. More than 500 stone steps lead to a simple monastery, its dry-stone buildings clinging to the cliff-edge, as they have done since the 7th century.

If you are unable to take the boat trip, drive across the causeway to **Valentia Island** to visit the **Skellig Experience Visitor Centre** ❼ (www.skellig experience.com; opening hours vary, check website for details), which introduces the Unesco-listed Skellig Michael and the other rocks.

Waterville

Return to the main Ring road and drive south 11km (7 miles) to **Waterville** ❽, a small resort famous for its golf course and the game angling on Lough Currane. Park in the centre near the Butler Arms and statue of Charlie Chaplin, who used to holiday here, and take a walk on the windswept sandy beach.

Derrynane House

Stop at the parking area on the **Coomakista Pass** ❾ to enjoy views of the

The Liberator

Daniel O'Connell (1775–1847), 'the Liberator', was born in Cahirciveen and adopted by an uncle from whom he inherited an estate at Derrynane. Landowner, lawyer and orator, he dominated Irish politics in the early 19th century. Educated in France, he introduced democracy to Ireland and was responsible for the Catholic Emancipation Act of 1829, allowing Catholics and Dissenters to vote, enter the professions and own land. Tall, burly and inexhaustible, O'Connell's immense appetite and physical stamina were legendary. He was no saint; he fought a fatal duel in his youth and had a reputation as a womaniser. Most Irish towns and villages have an O'Connell Street, including Dublin.

Sneem

Muckross Traditional Farms   *Ladies' View, Killarney*

Skelligs to the west and the mountains of the Beara Peninsula to the south.

In **Caherdaniel** drive downhill to **Derrynane House and National Park** ⑩ (http://derrynanehouse.ie; mid-Mar–early Nov daily 10am–5.15pm), family home of Daniel O'Connell. The modest 1702 manor house is furnished with heirlooms. Walk along the sheltered beach and explore the rock pools.

Killarney

Killarney National Park is a car-free zone and Muckross Park is at its core. Hire a jaunting car (open horse-drawn carriage) at the park gates: the park has wild deer, walking trails, a lakeside manor and Muckross Traditional Farms (www.muckross-house.ie; June–Aug daily 10am–6pm, May and Sept 1–6pm, Mar, Apr and Oct Sat–Sun 1–6pm), a beguiling outdoor museum of rural life.

For a quintessential Killarney experience, take a half-day Gap of Dunloe tour (O'Connor Autotours, Ross Road, Killarney; www.oconnorautotours.ie; May–Oct), which proceed on a pony and trap or on foot through 6.5km (4 miles) of narrow, unpaved mountain passes past huge glacial boulders, returning to town by boat. End the day by watching the sun set over the lakes from the 7th-century monastic ruins at Aghadoe. Killarney's Tourist Information Office is on Beech Road.

KENMARE RIVER

The Kenmare River is a sea inlet that divides the Iveragh Peninsula from the Beara Peninsula in the south.

Sneem

Brightly painted **Sneem** ⑪ has two village greens; park by the second. Walk down the road beyond the Blue Bull (signposted 'Pier') for about 300 metres/yds past an attractive garden. Looking back through the reeds you can appreciate Sneem's sheltered location between the sea and the hills. Note the difference in vegetation on this side of the Ring; in the place of bare windswept rocks is a lush growth of trees and shrubs.

Kenmare

Follow the N70 east for 27km (17 miles) to **Kenmare** ⑫. Laid out in 1755 in a triangle, the compact village is packed with restaurants, boutiques and crafts shops. Park in its centre beside the green and the **Kenmare Heritage Centre**, which introduces the town's history.

Food and Drink

① THE BRIDGE BAR

Portmagee; tel: 066-947 7108; www.moorings.ie; 9am–8.30pm; €
The simply prepared fish is leaping fresh; alternatively, opt for the roast of the day.

THE DINGLE PENINSULA

Jutting out into the Atlantic, the Dingle Peninsula is Europe's most westerly point. The Irish-speaking area at its tip is rich in prehistoric and early Christian remains, and has rugged cliffs and sandy beaches. Finish by crossing the sensational Conor Pass to Tralee, capital of County Kerry.

DISTANCE: 125km (77.5 miles)
TIME: A full day
START: Castlemaine
END: Tralee
POINTS TO NOTE: There is a daily bus service from Tralee to Dingle town, but really a car is essential for this route. Avoid the Conor Pass in misty weather; take the N86 from Dingle all the way to Tralee.

Begin at Castlemaine, the southern gateway to the Dingle Peninsula (Corca Dhuibhne), which stretches for some 48km (30 miles) from Tralee in the east to Slea Head in the west.

CASTLEMAINE TO DINGLE

Some 10km (6 miles) beyond **Castlemaine ❶**, the sea comes into view as the road skirts Castlemaine Harbour. The first hint of the scenery to come is at **Inch ❷**, where a 6.5km (4-mile) long sand spit backed by dunes stretches out into Dingle Bay. Stop for a bracing walk along the unusual west-facing beach and refuel at **Sammy's**, see ❶.

Annascaul

The wide road at **Annascaul ❸**, where the Castlemaine and Tralee roads meet, was once the location of a major cattle fair, which is also why this tiny village has so many pubs. One such pub, the **South Pole Inn**, was built by Tom Crean (1877–1938), a local man of legendary strength who enlisted in the Royal Navy and served on three Antarctic expeditions, with both Scott and Shackleton. The pub is crammed with fascinating memorabilia, and you can enjoy a view of green hills and grazing sheep from its front door.

Dingle town and harbour

From Annascaul, it's 17km (10.5 miles) west to **Dingle ❹** (An Daingean). Turn left at the entrance and park on the pier. Dingle has a population of about 1,500, which can treble in summer. Its fame was spread by the filming of *Ryan's Daughter* in 1969, and again in 1983 by the arrival of a dolphin, Fungie, who still plays in the harbour mouth. A

Dingle Harbour

bronze statue on the pier pays homage to the wild visitor. Opposite, in a humble tin shed, is one of Dingle's best seafood restaurants, **Out of the Blue**, see ➋.

A triangular 10-minute walk from the pier up Green Street, down Main Street and back along the Mall will take you past most of the town's shops and restaurants. The better craft shops are at the top of Green Street. Across the road from the pier you will find **Chowder Café**, see ➌.

SLEA HEAD DRIVE

Head west for 6km (3.75 miles) on the R559 to **Ventry** ➎ (Ceann Trá), an Irish-speaking village with a few pubs and shops. The bay here has a long sandy beach and safe swimming.

Between Ventry and Slea Head there are over 400 small conical huts of un-mortared stone known as beehive huts. While some date from the

5th–8th centuries and were used by hermit monks, many were built in the early 20th century to house farm implements; timber is so scarce here that it is cheaper to build with stone.

Dunbeg Fort

About 6km (3.75 miles) further, stop at the distinctive Stone House Restaurant at **Fahan** to visit **Dunbeg Promontory Fort** (www.dunbegfort.com; Apr–Oct daily 10am–5pm), a defensive promontory fort that was inhabited during about 800–1200AD. A short film introduces the compact site, which has an inner drystone rampart and a souterrain. It is perched right on the cliff's edge, reached by a short downhill path beside a field grazed by donkeys. About 250 metres/yds on, park again to visit a group of **beehive huts** above the road. In fine weather you can look south across the sea to the Skellig Rocks, where hardy monks lived in similar shelters.

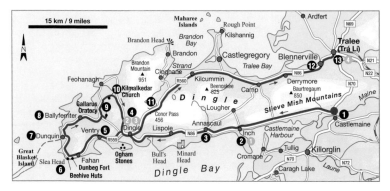

Ventry bay

Slea Head

The road climbs west around Eagle Mountain to **Slea Head** ❻ (Ceann Sléibhe), marked by a life-size roadside Crucifixion. **Coumenole**, the sandy beach below, will be familiar from *Ryan's Daughter*. It looks tempting, but swimming here is dangerous.

Dunquin and the Blasket Islands

Nearby **Dunquin** ❼ (Dún Chaoin) is a scattered settlement, as was the tradition in old Gaelic Ireland. The **Great Blasket** (An Blascaod Mór) is the largest of seven islands visible offshore. It was inhabited until 1953 by a tough, self-sufficient community of farmers and fishermen. The **Blasket Centre** (www.blasket.ie; Apr–mid-Oct daily 10am–6pm) at Dunquin explains the islanders' heritage. From **Dunquin Pier** (www.blasketisland.com) you can catch a ferry to the island.

Gallarus Oratory

Continue on the R559 for 7km (4.7 miles) to Irish-speaking **Ballyferriter** ❽ (Baile an Fheirtéaraigh), the largest village (two shops and four pubs that serve simple food) on this side of the peninsula, founded by the Norman Ferriter family in the 12th century and popular today with holidaymakers and Irish-language enthusiasts.

Some 8km (5 miles) further on is the **Gallarus Oratory** ❾ (www.gallarusoratory.ie). This extraordinary 8th-century building of unmortared stone is shaped like an inverted boat, and remains as dry and solid as the day it was built.

At the crossroads north of Gallarus, turn right (east) for the ruined **Kilmalkedar Church** ❿. It was built around 1150, although the settlement dates from the 7th century. The superbly carved Romanesque features have hardly weathered over the years. There are a number of interesting standing stones nearby, including a sundial stone and several Ogham stones, carved with letters from an early medieval alphabet.

CONOR PASS TO TRALEE

Return to Dingle on the R559 (8km/5 miles). If the weather is fine, drive to Tralee via the **Conor Pass** ⓫ (48km/ 30 miles), a rocky mountain road that crosses the peninsula from south to north. It rises steeply to 456 metres (1,496ft) above sea level, and parts are so narrow that you must negotiate right of way with oncoming traffic. It is not for the faint-hearted, but it does offer spectacular vistas of Brandon Bay and the wide Atlantic Ocean in the north; stop in a lay-by to enjoy the view. The road then corkscrews down to the bay, past a dazzling waterfall and boulder-strewn hillsides studded with glittering lakes.

Blennerville

There are glimpses of the sea as you drive along the R560 and join the N86

Slea Head

at **Camp**. **Blennerville** ⑫ is a mainly Georgian village perched between Tralee Bay and the old ship canal. It still has a large working windmill, best viewed from a distance.

Tralee

County town of Kerry, **Tralee** ⑬ (Trá Lí) has a population of more than 35,000, many of whom are students. Park in the centre near the town park beside **Ashe Memorial Hall**, an imposing neo-classical building housing the **Tourist Information Office**. The front entrance leads to the **Kerry County Museum** (www.kerrymuseum.ie; June–Aug daily 9.30am–5.30pm, Sept–May Tue–Sat until 5pm), with a lively display of Kerry's history from ancient times. Denny Street leads from the museum to the centre and contains the best of Tralee's Georgian architecture, mostly now lawyers' offices. A pedestrian alley on the left of Denny Street leads to Tralee's pedestrian piazza, which usually has a few market stalls trading. If you are in need of refreshment, try **The Grand Hotel**, see ④, back on Denny Street.

Food and Drink

① SAMMY'S CAFÉ
Inch Beach; tel: 066-915 8118; www.sammysinchbeach.com; daily 9.30am–10pm (weekends only Dec–Jan); €
This café-bar has an amazing beach location. By day it serves fresh salads, burgers, soups and sandwiches; at night it's fish and steaks.

② OUT OF THE BLUE
The Pier, Dingle town; tel: 066-915 0811; www.outoftheblue.ie; daily 5–10pm, Sun also 12.30–3pm; closed Nov–Feb; €€€
It's a basic tin hut beside the pier, but it serves the freshest of seafood cooked to perfection. Book in advance.

③ CHOWDER CAFÉ
Strand Street, Dingle town; tel: 066-915 1061; daily 10am–5pm, June–Sept Tue–Sat also 6–9pm; €€
A simple café where bread, cakes and desserts are home-made. There are good vegetarian and gluten-free options. Dishes include steaks, lamb shank and excellent chips.

④ THE GRAND HOTEL
Denny Street, Tralee; tel: 066-712 1499; www.grandhoteltralee.com; daily: bar food served 8.30am–9.30pm, restaurant 7.30–10am, 12.30–2.30pm, 6–9.30pm; €€
This fine old institution has an imposing Victorian facade. In the Pikeman's Bar there are good-value specials at the self-service lunch like roast leg of lamb and sea trout fillet. More formal food is served in the evening in Samuel's Restaurant.

Thatched cottage, Adare

LIMERICK AND SHANNON

On this route, explore the charming village of Adare, wander the medieval streets of Limerick and then head into the castle country around the Shannon estuary to discover more of Ireland's past at Bunratty Castle and Folk Park.

DISTANCE: 71km (44 miles)
TIME: A full day
START: Adare
END: Quin
POINTS TO NOTE: Adare is on the N21, 7km (4 miles) west of the N20 Cork–Limerick road and 17km (10 miles) southwest of Limerick city. From Quin, return to the N18, where you can head south for Limerick (34km/21 miles) or north for Lahinch (38km/23 miles), the starting point of route 11.

The Limerick region and the Shannon estuary have been of great strategic importance ever since the Vikings established a sheltered seaport on an island at the head of the Shannon estuary in the 9th century, which grew into the city of Limerick. During the 12th–15th centuries several monastic orders settled in the area, while Irish clan chieftains built fortified homes among the low hills and lakes to the northwest of Limerick. This castle country is dotted with the ruins of tower houses,

some of which have been restored, such as Craggaunowen and magnificent Bunratty Castle.

ADARE

Begin the day to the southwest of Limerick city at **Adare ❶**, which boasts of being 'Ireland's prettiest village'. It's a tiny place

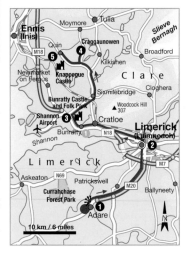

Augustinian friary, Adare

Idyllic Adare

and you cannot miss the **Adare Heritage Centre** (Main Street; www.adareheritage centre.ie; daily 9am–5pm) at its heart. There is a large car park behind the centre, plus several crafts shops and a restaurant within. You can pick up a map of the village here.

Main Street

Turn left out of the Heritage Centre to the former **Trinitarian priory**, founded in 1230; it was converted into a Catholic parish church in 1811. The opposite side of the wide main street is lined by thatched cottages with flower-filled front gardens. They were built in 1830 by the local landlord, the Earl of Dunraven, for his workers. Today, most of them are either restaurants or craft shops. **Lucy Erridge's** is the most interesting of the latter.

Augustinian friary

Turn left out of the Dunraven Arms, which marks the end of the village, and continue for about 50 metres/yds to the former **Augustinian friary**, now Adare's Anglican church. To the north of the church are the well-preserved cloisters of the 1315 monastery. The church's nave and choir are also 14th-century.

The main gates of **Adare Manor** (www.adaremanor.com; closed for refurbishment until Autumn 2017) are across the road from the church. The manor, which was enlarged in the Tudor Revival style in the mid-19th century, is now a luxury hotel and golf resort.

River walk

At this point you could go through the metal stile beside the Anglican church for a lovely rural riverside walk of about 1.5km (1 mile). The walk follows the banks of the River Maigue, rich in wildlife, to the west, before looping back to the village centre down Station Road.

LIMERICK CITY

Leaving Adare for **Limerick** ❷ takes you out of a cosy time warp and into modern Ireland, with a dual carriageway (N20) approaching the Republic's third largest city. The bulk of the low-lying city is positioned on the eastern bank of the River Shannon, and the wide, fast-flowing river is its best asset.

Follow signs for the centre and Arthur's Quay car park; behind is the **Tourist Information Centre** (www. limerick.ie; Mon–Sat 9am–5pm, July–Aug daily). Both the Shannon and, to the east, King John's Castle, can be seen from here.

Hunt Museum

Turn right up Francis Street and left into Rutland Street for the **Hunt Museum** Ⓐ (www.huntmuseum.com; Mon–Sat 10am–5pm, Sun 2–5pm). Once the city's Custom House, the compact Georgian building has the finest collection of Celtic and medieval treasures outside Dublin's National Museum, plus a small selection of Irish and European paintings, including works by

King John's Castle, Limerick

Renoir and Picasso. Once a private collection, it was donated to the nation in 1976 by the Hunt family. There's also a shop and an excellent café overlooking the river.

St Mary's Cathedral

Turn left upon leaving the Hunt Museum and cross a bridge over a tributary of the Shannon to **King's Island**, site of the city's original settlement. On the left is **St Mary's Cathedral ⓑ** (Mon–Fri 9.30am–4.30pm, Sun services only). The rounded Romanesque entrance door is a remnant of its origins as a 12th-century palace belonging to Donal Mór O'Brien, King of Munster. Much of the compact cruciform building dates from the 15th-century, such as the black-oak misericords with carved animal features in the choir stalls.

King John's Castle

From the cathedral turn onto Nicholas Street and walk north for **King John's Castle ⓒ** (www.shannonheritage.com; daily Apr–Sept 9.30am–5.30pm, Oct–Mar until 4.30pm), a massive fortification with curtain walls and two drum towers, built by the Normans in the 1200s and rebuilt and extended many times over the years. The outdoor courtyard gives access to the massive bastions and views of the river and city. Reopened in June 2013 following major investment, King John's Castle has a new visitor centre and exhibition that brings to life its dramatic history through 21st-century technology.

Riverside footpath

Turn right out of the castle, and right again down a pedestrian alley beside the castle walls, past the **Jim Kemmy Municipal Museum** (Tue–Sat 10am–1pm, 2.15–5pm; free), to return to the car park along a riverside footpath. At Merchant's Quay look for the modern white footbridge across the river.

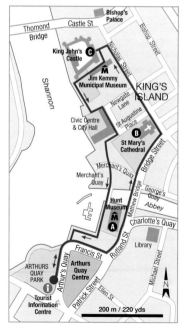

St Mary's Cathedral doorway   *Hunt Museum*

NORTH OF LIMERICK CITY

Cross the River Shannon in County Clare via the N18, the road to Shannon Airport and the west of Ireland.

Bunratty Castle and Folk Park

Impressively big, **Bunratty Castle** ❸ (www.shannonheritage.com; daily 9am–5.30pm) has a square tower at each corner and a drawbridge. Dating largely from the 16th-century, it contains furniture and tapestries from the 14th–17th centuries. In the evening Bunratty hosts 'medieval banquets' – a meal with Irish cabaret and plenty of 'Blarney'.

The extensive **Folk Park** (as above with last entry 4.15pm) consists of 10ha (25 acres) of reconstructed traditional dwellings, including a typical village street c.1880, complete with pecking hens. The original of many an 'Irish pub', **Durty Nelly's** squats on the riverbank beside the castle. It does not serve food in the daytime, so turn right out of Bunratty Castle and after a short way you will see **J.P. Clarke's Country Pub**, see ①.

Craggaunowen – the Living Past Experience

Take the narrow country lane behind J.P. Clarke's to the T-junction with the R471 and turn right for **Sixmilebridge**. Drive through the village and turn left onto the R469 for Craggaunowen, well signposted about 10km (6 miles) from Bunratty. Among the attractions at **Craggaunowen – the Living Past**

Experience ❹ (www.shannonheritage.com; Easter–Aug daily 10am–5pm) are a restored 1550 castle and a reconstructed *crannóg*, a fortified dwelling of clay and wattle built on a lake island. Come and explore the roots of the people, homesteads, animals and artefacts of our Celtic ancestors.

Quin

Retrace your steps from Craggaunowen and turn west onto the R469 for about 4km (2.5 miles) to **Quin** ❺. In the village centre are the well-preserved remains of a **Franciscan abbey**, founded in 1402, with cloisters and elaborate stone tombs. Across the stream are the ruins of a 13th-century church.

Drive across the village's bridge, and take the first left, a narrow country road which meanders for about 5km (3 miles) to an interchange with the N18.

THE CLIFFS OF MOHER AND THE BURREN

Drive along County Clare's attractive coast to the dramatic Cliffs of Moher, which rise vertically from the Atlantic, and the eerie Burren, a treeless limestone plateau that fascinates botanists, geologists and archaeologists.

DISTANCE: 78km (48.5 miles)
TIME: A full day
START: Lahinch
END: Kinvara
POINTS TO NOTE: Lahinch is also spelt Lehinch. It is 30km (18.5 miles) west of Ennis on the N85. Kinvara is 10km (6 miles) west of the N18 Galway–Limerick road and 30km (19 miles) south of Galway city (route 12).

Lahinch, on the west coast of County Clare, has long been famous for its golf links and is now also one of Ireland's most popular surfing destinations. The huge bulk of the Cliffs of Moher rise 200 metres (650ft) straight out of the sea on this coast and stretch for some 7km (4 miles), offering distant views of the Aran Islands and close-up ones of nesting seabirds. To the north, the Burren is a National Park covering 500 sq km (200 sq miles) of lunar-like limestone pavement, with unique flora and fauna and numerous megalithic remains, dating from the Stone Age and

the Bronze Age, long before the arrival of the Celts.

LAHINCH TO LISCANNOR

The driving route begins with a right turn just before **Lahinch ❶** (approaching from Ennis), but first carry straight on, turning right off the main road at the top of the village to park above the long sandy beach, where you can take a walk along its promenade. These days surfers may even outnumber golfers, and the village has a lively nightlife.

Return to the R478. The road curves north to west through the golf links and a series of sand dunes, with intermittent sea views.

Liscannor

The tiny village of **Liscannor ❷** nearby is somewhat overwhelmed by newly built holiday homes, but still has an excellent pub at its centre, **Vaughan's Anchor Inn**, see ❶. The village has given its name to a black stone, Liscannor slate, usually used as flagstones, which bear the fossil remains of marine

animals that lived up to 300 million years ago. In the early 20th century, more than 500 men were employed in local quarries.

As you head to the Cliffs of Moher, look out for **The Rock Shop** (www.therockshop.ie; daily 10am–5pm), which has interesting audio-visual displays about quarrying and a collection of antique tools, plus a nice tearoom.

THE CLIFFS OF MOHER

The exhilarating **Cliffs of Moher** ❸ attract over a million visitors a year. Park at the multi-million-euro **Visitor Centre** (www.cliffsofmoher.ie; daily Nov–Feb 9am–5pm, Mar, Oct until 6pm, Apr until 6.30pm, May and Sept until 7pm, June until 7.30pm, July–Aug until 9pm), which is built into the hillside and roofed with grass. It contains a shop, ATM and café, plus the **Atlantic Edge Exhibition**, the highlight of which is a virtual reality tour of the cliffs from a bird's-eye view. In good weather, harpists and other buskers entertain outside. Note the extensive use of the local Liscannor stone as paving and seating.

The cliffs

Part of the recent investment in the Cliffs of Moher included an upgrading of over 600 metres/yds of pathways and viewing platforms to enable visitors to enjoy the spectacle safely and without harming the area's wildlife and ecological balance. The natural layering of the rocks creates ledges that are an ideal habitat for nesting seabirds, including fulmars, kittiwakes, razorbills and puffins. The breeding season runs from May to July. For the full wind-swept experience, go right up to the edge and watch the waves booming far below. In clear weather you can see the Aran Islands and the far side of Liscannor Bay.

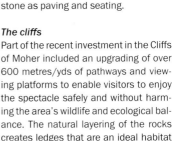

THE BURREN

The road now winds through the heart of the Burren, a treeless plateau with swirling lime-

Cracked limestone of the Burren

stone terraces, huge rocks erratically deposited in the Ice Age and relics of prehistoric man, including cairns, court graves, dolmens and more than 400 stone forts. The land once had a thin covering of soil, but time, weather and the farming activities of prehistoric man denuded the surface, leaving the lunar-like region seen today. Meanwhile, under the ground, acid in the rainwater has seeped through the limestone to create pools and caves. Some 125 types of plant from Alpine, Arctic and Mediterranean zones flourish here, often growing up through the rock; they are at their best in May.

Kilfenora

The R478 crosses the N67 outside Lisdoonvarna and becomes the R476, continuing for 9km (5.5 miles) to another tiny village, **Kilfenora ❹**. Here, **St Fachtnan's Cathedral** is an attractive little 12th-century church with some finely carved effigies and three medieval high crosses. Next door, **The Burren Centre** (www.theburrencentre.ie; mid-Mar–Oct daily 10am–5pm, until 5.30pm in summer) has a short film introducing the unique landscape of the Burren.

Leamaneh Castle

Continuing east, the left turn onto the R480 has an unmissable landmark, the beautifully proportioned ruins of **Leamaneh Castle ❺**. It is not open to the public and the surrounding lands are grazed by cattle. Close up, you can see that it was built in two phases: the tower in 1480 and the manor in 1640.

Poulnabrone Dolmen

The road between here and Ballyvaughan abounds in megalithic remains. A stone-walled car park has been built to accommodate visitors at the **Poulnabrone Dolmen ❻**, a structure over 3 metres (10ft) high and the Burren's finest portal tomb, dating back to 2,500BC.

Aillwee Caves

The road then winds downhill through a series of corkscrew bends, with distant sea views, to **Aillwee Caves ❼** (www.aillweecave.ie; daily 10am–5.30/6pm). Fronted by a massive shop and flanked by a separate birds of prey attraction,

---

The Burren Way

The Burren Way runs from Ballyvaughan to Liscannor, a distance of 45km (26.5 miles). The terrain varies from rocky ground where only scrub grows to magnificent wide 'green paths', and is largely off road. Part of the route runs along the top of the Cliffs of Moher, with great views of the Aran Islands. As well as a wealth of wildflowers, you might well glimpse some of the Burren fauna, which includes wild goats, foxes, hares, rabbits, badgers, the rare pine marten (*martes martes*) and a rich diversity of butterfly species.

Dunguaire Castle

this is one of the few Burren caves accessible to the public. The guided tour takes you about 300 metres/yds through narrow passages into chambers with vast stalactites and past waterfalls.

AROUND GALWAY BAY

The road skirts the southern shore of Galway Bay, a sheltered, indented coastline, and in good weather there are views of the purple hills of Connemara on the opposite shore.

Ballyvaughan

A small fishing village on the southern shore of Galway Bay with plenty of accommodation, **Ballyvaughan** ❽ is the starting point of the **Burren Way** way-marked walk and a popular base for walkers and scholarly visitors to the **National Park** (www.burrennational park.ie) on the southeastern side of the Burren. **Monk's Bar**, see ❷, is a waterside bar with good food.

Kinvara

The road east out of Ballyvaughan skirts the shore of Galway Bay, and to the right offers stunning views of the grey, rocky heights of the Burren. **Kinvara** ❾, 20km (12 miles) east, at the top of the sheltered inlet of **Kinvara Bay**, is the kind of quiet fishing village that can steal your heart away. Turn left down the road beside the Merriman Hotel and right along its harbour to see it at its best. Kinvara is also known for the traditional music played here.

Dunguaire Castle

Magnificently sited on a rock, **Dunguaire Castle** (www.shannonheritage.com; mid-Apr–Oct daily 10am–4pm, last entry 4.30pm) looks out to sea on the northern side of Kinvara Bay. Built in 1520, it has been fully restored, and hosts medieval banquets in the evening (Apr–Oct; book in advance).

Flags in Eyre Square

GALWAY

A half-day route around the medieval centre of Galway, the main urban hub of the west of Ireland and a vibrant fast-growing city with a young population and distinctive Irish identity.

DISTANCE: About 1km (0.5 mile)
TIME: A half day
START/END: Eyre Square
POINTS TO NOTE: Galway city is 27km (17 miles) southeast of Oughterard, the starting point of route 13, on the N59.

Galway city is situated where the River Corrib flows into the Atlantic Ocean. Its commercial centre is compact, largely pedestrianised and packed with quaint shops, trendy boutiques, stylish cafés and lively pubs.

Galway escaped the attention of the Vikings, thus retaining its Irish customs until the Anglo-Norman invasion in the 13th century. The invaders built a walled town, which developed as a thriving port. They traded in wine, spices and fish, forging strong links with Spain, rather than England and Wales, due to the town's westerly location. It became known as 'the City of the Tribes', as 14 powerful Anglo-Norman merchant families controlled its wealth for many centuries. Remnants of their stone-built mansions can still be seen in the city's narrow lanes and cobbled streets.

EYRE SQUARE TO THE RIVER CORRIB

Begin at **Eyre Square ❶**, site of the **J.F. Kennedy Park** and city's focal point. In the northern corner 14 flags, each representing one of the merchant tribes, stand alongside the **Quincentennial Fountain ❷**, erected in 1984 to mark Galway's 500th anniversary as a city. Its rust-coloured 'sails' depict those of the Galway hooker, a traditional wooden cargo boat. The **Tourist Information Office** (www.galwaytourism.ie) is in Forster Street off the eastern corner.

The northwestern side of Eyre Square leads into **Williamsgate Street** (look for the landmark **Brown Thomas** department store; www.brownthomas. com). This street is the spine of old Galway and changes its name four times before reaching the River Corrib.

Market near Church of St Nicholas

Lynch's Castle

At the junction of William Street and Shop Street, the Allied Irish Bank occupies one of Galway's oldest buildings, **Lynch's Castle ❸**, a 15th-century fortified townhouse. Note the cheeky gargoyles, Lynch family arms and the carved stone panels on its facade. Inside, a 1651 map shows Galway's street layout, little changed today.

Collegiate Church of St Nicholas

Continue south and follow the next fork to the right, leading to the **Collegiate Church of St Nicholas ❹**, founded in 1320 and now the Church of Ireland (Episcopalian) cathedral. There is a popular belief that Christopher Columbus prayed here in 1477 before setting off to discover America. The area around the church has a vibrant Saturday market.

A signpost will direct you to Bowling Green and the **Nora Barnacle House ❺** (mid-May–mid-Sept 10am–1pm, 2–5pm), Ireland's smallest museum and family home of James Joyce's wife.

Quay Street

Return to the central spine via Lombard Street. On the corner of Cross Street and Quay Street is **Tigh Neachtain ❻** (Noctan's; tel: 091-568820; http://tighneachtain.com), one of Galway's oldest and most traditional pubs, with a warren-like wood-clad interior. It is also the unofficial information point for the city's busy arts scene.

To the left, on High Street, look for a sign to the pretty **Old Malte Mall**. To the right, on Quay Street, traditional shops selling tweeds and Aran sweaters prosper alongside vintage and designer clothing boutiques and contemporary arts-and-crafts galleries, a scene enlivened by an international array of buskers. Most bars and

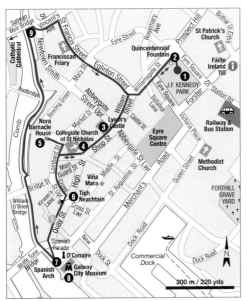

Quayside houses in Galway

restaurants here, including **McDonagh's**, see ❶, have outside tables.

ALONG THE CORRIB

Quay Street reaches the Corrib at the open space of Spanish Parade. Turn left for the **Spanish Arch** ❼, named after the city's former trading partner. Beside is the modern **Galway City Museum** ❽ (www.galwaycitymuseum.ie; Tue–Sat 10am–5pm, Sun noon–5pm; free). Large flocks of swans congregate here and there are usually a few Galway hookers moored on the opposite bank.

Riverside walk

Cross the road at Wolfe Tone Bridge and follow the footpath along this side of the river, past the William O'Brien Bridge all the way to the **Salmon Weir Bridge** ❾. From mid-April to early July, you can spot shoals of salmon lying in the water before making their way upstream to Lough Corrib to spawn. Cross the bridge to visit Galway's 20th-century **Catholic Cathedral** before crossing back and taking the second right onto St Francis Street, which becomes Eglinton Street and leads towards Eyre Square.

Aran Islands

The Aran Islands – Inishmore (Inis Mór), Inishman (Inis Meain) and Inisheer (Inis Oirr) – are strung across the mouth of Galway Bay. They contain many archaeological remains; the biggest is Inishmore's Dun Aengus (Dún Aoinghusa), a 2,000-year-old Celtic fort perched on a 90-metre (300ft) sheer cliff. The islands' wildlife is unusually rich, and walkers will enjoy the Atlantic air and narrow paths that run between tiny fields. Inishmore is the most popular; go to Inishman or Inisheer for solitude. Irish is the islanders' first language, but all speak English too.

Wait until arrival to book, so you can vary your plans according to the weather. Ferries from Rossaveal take an hour and there are bus connections to Galway city. Aran Island Ferries (www.aranislandferries.com) has daily sailings (€25 return). Aer Arann (www.aerarannislands.ie) operates daily flights year round from Connemara Regional Airport in Inverin (€49 return). Shop around for deals including bed and breakfast; if possible, spend at least a night on an island for the full experience.

Food and Drink

❶ MCDONAGH'S SEAFOOD HOUSE

22 Quay Street; tel: 091-565001; www.mcdonaghs.net; restaurant Mon–Sat 5–10pm, chip bar Mon–Sat noon–11pm, Sun 2–9pm; €€

A self-service chippy on one side and a seafood restaurant on the other, McDonagh's is a Galway institution. The chippy also offers seafood chowder and a selection of seafood salads.

Windswept bog

CONNEMARA

Drive across sparsely inhabited, lake–studded bogland, with huge skies above, mountains ahead and hospitable villages en route. Highlights include the attractive town of Clifden, Connemara National Park, the romantic 19th–century Kylemore Abbey and the deep–water fjord at Killary Harbour.

DISTANCE: 86km (53.5 miles)
TIME: A full day
START: Oughterard
END: Leenane
POINTS TO NOTE: Oughterard is 27km (17 miles) west of Galway on the N59 Clifden road. Leenane is also on the N59, 32km (20 miles) south of Westport, the starting point of route 14. Note that Killary Cruises offers its best rates for touring Killary Harbour if you book online.

Stretching from Galway Bay in the south to Killary Harbour in the north, bordered by a rocky coastline and consisting mainly of rugged hills, windswept bogs and innumerable lakes, Connemara has always been an isolated place. Oscar Wilde described it as a 'savage beauty', and it remains relatively untamed. Its southern coast is home to Ireland's largest Gaeltacht (Irish-speaking area), while in north and central Connemara (covered by this route) there are still more sheep than people; traditionally, people lived by the sea where subsistence farming could be augmented by fishing. The central area has largely escaped unsightly new developments, while existing attractions have been quietly enhanced.

LOUGH CORRIB

Oughterard ❶ (pronounced 'ookterard'), a village about 40 minutes' drive from Galway, grew up chiefly to accommodate anglers heading for Lough Corrib and consists largely of tackle shops, souvenir shops and small hotels. To orient yourself, on arriving in Oughterard turn right at the Esso petrol station for a 1km (0.5 mile) detour to the pier on **Lough Corrib** ❷. Here you can gauge the scale of the lough, which covers 17,000ha (42,000 acres) and is over 43km (26 miles) long. This is one of its widest points, at 22.5km (14 miles); Cong in County Mayo is on the opposite shore. Today, the lough mainly attracts anglers, but in the past it was an important conduit for turf, lime, grain and seaweed to and from Galway docks.

Clifden

Cruise of the lough

Corrib Cruises (tel: 091-557 768; www.
corribcruises.com; June–Aug Wed–
Mon, noon; phone in advance to confirm) offers short tours of the lough from
the pier as well as a day trip to **Inchago-
ill Island**, a romantic spot which has
interesting remains of two churches
dating from the 12th and 13th centuries. The cruise continues to Cong, then
returns directly to Oughterard.

On the western side of Oughterard
is a pretty wooded stretch with a **river
walk** beside the Owenriff. Enjoy the
trees; they are the last you will see for
many miles.

INTO CONNEMARA

About 2km (1 mile) west of Oughterard
the real wilderness scenery begins:
low-lying plains, scattered blue lakes
and a line of distant mountains under
an enormous sky usually hung with
large clouds. The plains are mostly
bog-land and in summer you will see
heaps of hand-cut turf drying at the
side of the road.

After another 14km (8.5 miles),
Maam Cross ❸ is more of a crossroads
than a village; the junction with the road
to Leenane and the northern shores of
Lough Corrib, it was an important place
for trading cattle in the old days. A large
agricultural fair is still held here every
year in August.

Clifden

The road continues for 14km (8.5
miles) to **Recess ❹**, another tiny ham-
let, with views in the distant north of
the Twelve Bens mountain range. After
another 20km (12.5 miles), the road
approaches **Clifden ❺**, Connemara's

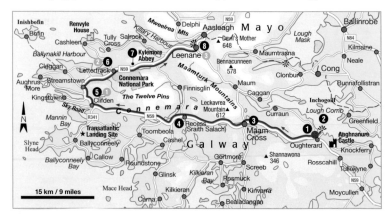

A hardy Connemara pony

main (and only) town. It is pleasantly sited, with two church spires under a wooded peak and above a sea inlet. A compact, lively place, lined with bars, cafés, bookshops and arts-and-crafts galleries, it attracts a wide range of visitors, from artists and hill climbers to Connemara pony enthusiasts. It also has a flourishing lobster fishery and a reputation for good food and comfortable lodgings. Such is its popularity that it has a one-way traffic system; go with the flow around two sides of a triangle, then park. Retrace your steps on foot to browse the shops and galleries. Look out for **Mitchell's Seafood Restaurant**, at the highest point of the triangle, see ❶.

A possible detour just south of Clifden on the R341 Ballyconneely road is a memorial commemorating the landing of the first transatlantic flight. On 15 June 1919 Alcock and Brown landed their wood and fabric-covered bi-plane nose-first into soft bog after flying for 16 hours and 12 minutes.

Sky Road

At the western end of Market Street the road forks at the Bank of Ireland. Take the right-hand fork uphill, past the Abbeyglen Hotel, for the **Sky Road**. After about 400 metres/yds, look back to see Clifden, with its twin spires and the backdrop of the Twelve Bens. The road continues to rise to about 150 metres (500ft), with views of the beach below the town and an exhilarating panorama of the islands off Clifden Bay and the open sea beyond. People often say it feels like being on the top of the world. You can opt to drive the 11km (7-mile) circuit on narrow, twisting roads, and re-join the N59 northwest of Clifden; this will add about half an hour to your journey.

NORTHERN CONNEMARA

Beyond Clifden, the N59 skirts for 15km (9 miles) around Connemara's western edge and turns east for **Letterfrack** ❻. The village has a few shops and bars, but the best place for a break is on the western approach at the **Avoca Craft Shop**, see ❷. Just beyond it is the **Connemara National Park Visitor Centre** (www.connemaranationalpark.ie; mid-Mar–Oct daily 9am–5.30pm; free). The park itself (open year round 9am–5.30pm) is not enclosed, but covers some 2,000ha (4,942 acres) of scenic wilderness. Trails have been marked out of varying degrees of difficulty. The Visitor Centre is a model of its kind, with displays on Connemara's history, fauna, flora and geology, a children's playground, a tea room and an indoor picnic area.

Kylemore Abbey

Nearby, **Kylemore Abbey** ❼ (www.kylemoreabbey.com; daily 10am–4.30pm), a massive limestone and granite neo-Gothic mansion with battlements above its numerous windows, rears up against

Kylemore Abbey

a wooded backdrop on the far side of a reedy lake. It was built in the 1860s by a wealthy local MP for his wife, who died tragically soon after and is commemorated by a tiny Gothic church. Since the 1920s, the building has been home to Benedictine nuns, who ran a prestigious girls' boarding school until 2010. The nuns have restored a large walled Victorian garden, accessible by minibus or forest walk. There's also a lovely lakeside walk.

Leenane and Killary Harbour

Leenane ❽ (Leenaun on Sat Nav) is at the inland end of **Killary Harbour**, Ireland's only fjord. On its southern shore, **Killary Cruises** (www.killarycruises.com; daily Apr–Oct) offers one and a half hour harbour trips and promises no seasickness – with a money-back guarantee.

In the village, turn left over the bridge to enjoy the long view down the harbour (so long that the sea at its mouth is obscured by mountains), and visit the **Sheep and Wool Centre** (www.sheepandwoolcentre.com; mid-Mar–Oct daily 9.30am–6pm). Here, the O'Toole family demonstrate traditional techniques of spinning, carding, dyeing and weaving wool, the main industry in Leenane a hundred years ago. Some fascinating photos show the village in those days. Introduced in 2013, sheepdog demonstrations can now be enjoyed as part of the museum visit. Walk back over the bridge to sample a real Irish pub, **Hamilton's Bar**, see ❾.

Food and Drink

❶ MITCHELL'S SEAFOOD RESTAURANT

Market Street, Clifden; 095-21867; www.mitchellsrestaurantclifden.com; Mar–Oct daily noon–10pm; €€

Stone walls, wooden floors and an open fire make an atmospheric restaurant of this former shop. Local mussels are steamed in garlic, while fresh crab is served on home-made bread. Meat eaters and vegetarians both have ample choice.

❷ AVOCA CRAFT SHOP

Letterfrack; tel: 095-41058; Mon–Fri 9.30am–5.30pm, Sat–Sun 10am–6pm; €

Before you even see the shop, the car park's picnic tables overlooking a sheltered sea inlet will tempt you to stop. Avoca's cafés are known for creating light, wholesome dishes, using local and artisan products. Do not miss the old-fashioned sweeties in the shop.

❸ HAMILTON'S BAR

Leenane; tel: 095-42266; Mon–Thu 11am–11.30pm, Fri–Sat until 12.30am, Sun until 11pm; €

This old-style pub has a grocery shop in the front, a pool table in the back and a pair of petrol pumps outside, as well as picnic tables. It serves home-made soup and fresh seafood (including open crab or salmon sandwiches).

Westport townhouses

WESTPORT AND MAYO

Explore the charms of Westport town, then explore County Mayo with a drive along island-studded Clew Bay to visit Croagh Patrick, Saint Patrick's Holy Mountain. Head inland to the National Museum of Country Life and Foxford Woollen Mills, returning via beautiful Lough Cullin.

DISTANCE: Circular route: 82km (51 miles)
TIME: 1-hour walk; a half-day drive
START/END: Westport
POINTS TO NOTE: Ballina is 16km (10 miles) north of Foxford, and it is 61km (38 miles) from Ballina to Sligo (route 15).

Mayo is a large county consisting mainly of bog and mountains, with a coastline battered by the Atlantic. It has long been synonymous with remoteness and poverty, but its unspoilt scenery has made it a popular destination for outdoor lovers.

WESTPORT

Westport ❶ is a compact town of considerable charm, where old Irish ways still prevail. Drive into the centre and park near the highest point. (There is a large car park at the top of Mill Street behind Navin Funeral Home.)

The Octagon and Mall

The town was designed in the late 18th century by John Browne, the Viscount Westport, to complement his new home, Westport House – making Westport one of just a few planned towns in Ireland. All roads lead to the **Octagon**, the town's marketplace. Around its eight sides are some cut-stone Georgian buildings and at its centre is a statue of Saint Patrick on a tall stone plinth.

Walk down James Street and cross the bridge to take a right on **North Mall**, a tree-lined thoroughfare that runs beside the canalised Carrowbeg River. Turn right at the next bridge up Bridge Street, which has a landmark **clock tower** at its top, as well as the **Tourist Information Office** (www.westporttourism.com). The town has a quirky mix of modern businesses and old traditional ones. Among the latter is a butcher's shop with an art gallery upstairs and a café, **McCormack's Café at the Andrew Stone Gallery**, see ❶.

Clew Bay and Westport House

Drive from the Octagon down Quay Hill to the **harbour**. The quays face

Westport, Clew Bay and Croaghpatrick

a beautiful stretch of calm water and the island-studded **Clew Bay**. Many of the old warehouses are now hotels and holiday apartments.

From the quays, turn right facing the water and follow the signs for about 200 metres/yds to reach **Westport House and Pirate Adventure Park** (www.westporthouse.ie; Mar–Oct daily 10am–6pm, with exceptions). The fine 18th-century house in the classical style has period furniture and paintings, but children prefer the funfair and adventure park, with Ireland's only plunge log-flume ride and swan-shaped pedalos on the lake. There is also a camping and caravan park.

CROAGH PATRICK

The R335 to **Murrisk ❷**, 5km (3 miles) west of Westport, is signposted from the quays. It is a scattered, sea-facing fishing village with two pubs; try **The Tavern Bar**, see ❷.

Beyond Murrisk is the car park for pilgrims who intend to climb the Holy Mountain, **Croagh Patrick ❸**, known locally as 'The Reek'. Here, the **Croagh Patrick Visitor Centre** (www.croagh-patrick.com) has a café, a craft shop, hot showers and secure lockers.

The cone-shaped peak is almost 800 metres (2,600ft) high and has a small oratory. This is where Saint Patrick is said to have rung his bell to summon Ireland's venomous creatures and cast them from the island. On the last Sunday in July about 30,000 pilgrims make the ascent, some of them barefoot. It takes a fit person about three hours there and back, and is well worth the effort for the views of Clew Bay.

Cross the road at the base of Croagh Patrick. Walk beyond a bronze sculpture, the centre-piece of the **Famine Memorial Park**; near the shoreline you will find **Murrisk Abbey**, a traditional starting point for the ascent of the Reek. The ruin of an Augustinian friary, founded in 1456, has some fine stonework in its eastern window.

Mayo sheep

National Famine Memorial, Murrisk

NORTH OF WESTPORT

Return to Westport and take the N5 east through Castlebar for 24km (16 miles) to Turlough.

National Museum of Country Life
The **National Museum of Country Life** ❹ (www.museum.ie; Tue–Sat 10am–5pm, Sun 2–5pm; free) in Turlough Park houses the National Folklife Collection, illustrating traditional ways of life in rural Ireland from 1850 to about 1950. The displays are hugely appealing to both young and old. The award-winning modern building is in the grounds of a former stately home, and there is a good shop and café here.

Foxford Woollen Mills
Follow the N5 east for about 5km (3 miles) and turn north at Bellavary for another 12km (7 miles) to **Foxford** ❺. Drive through the village to find the **Foxford Woollen Mills Visitor Centre** (www. foxfordwoollenmills.com; Mon–Sat 10am–5pm, Sun noon–5pm). The mill was founded in 1892 to relieve poverty by a remarkable nun; Foxford is known for high-quality tweeds, rugs and blankets. Afterwards, you could make a stop at **Poacher's Bar and Restaurant**, see ❸.

Pontoon
Cross the bridge over the River Moy and take the R318 west for 7km (4 miles) to **Pontoon** ❻. Stop at the car park for a great view of Lough Cullin, surrounded by low hills. Pontoon is not a village as such, but a landbridge dividing Lough Cullin from Lough Conn in the north. Turn left on to the R310 to cross it, enjoying views of water on either side.

Return to Castlebar on R310, an almost uninhabited route with thriving birdlife (such as snipe and woodcock), and take the N5 west back to Westport.

Food and Drink

❶ MCCORMACK'S CAFÉ AT THE ANDREW STONE GALLERY
Bridge Street, Westport; tel: 098-25619; Thu–Sat, Mon 10.15am–4.45pm; €
Cakes, quiches and pâtés are displayed in a cold counter, and there are hot specials like bacon and cabbage, or lamb casserole.

❷ THE TAVERN BAR
Murrisk; tel: 098-64060; www.tavern murrisk.com; Sun–Thu 12.30–11pm, Fri–Sat until 12.30am; €
Local fishermen used to arrive here with buckets of langoustines. The menu also includes a selection of cheeses and meat.

❸ POACHER'S BAR AND RESTAURANT
Main Street, Foxford; tel: 094-925 6518; www.mayflyhotel.com; food served Mon–Sat 8am–9pm, Sun noon–9pm; €€
This bar and restaurant in the Mayfly Hotel offers traditional Irish cooking and a convivial atmosphere. A favourite of visiting anglers.

Rosses Point

SLIGO AND DONEGAL

*The counties of Sligo and Donegal are stunningly beautiful. County Sligo
has a famous literary heritage, awe-inspiring scenery and fabulous beaches,
while County Donegal has a quiet, but breathtaking, magnificence.*

DISTANCE: 100km (62miles)
TIME: 1 or 2 days
START: Sligo town
END: Donegal town
POINTS TO NOTE: If you are staying
in Sligo town, you could return there
after visiting Mullaghmore, rather than
continuing on to Donegal town. If you
are planning to climb Knocknarea,
consider an overnight stay. The best
way to Belfast from Donegal is via
Omagh and Lisburn. Drive via Derry/
Londonderry to visit the Giant's
Causeway en route.

County Sligo's dramatically carved
coastal scenery is a formidable reminder
of the last ice age. This route takes in
some of the county's scenic highlights,
including Knocknarea mountain and
Lough Gill, as well as the literary highlights of Yeats country, before winding
north along the coast towards windswept
Mullaghmore, the beaches of County
Donegal and bustling Donegal town.
Linked to the Republic by a slender isth-

mus, much of Donegal harks back to a
remote, rural age. For some here, Irish
Gaelic is their first language and, as you
head further west into the Gaeltacht
area, road signs are written first in Irish
and second in English.

SLIGO TOWN

Pretty **Sligo town ❶** is set on the banks of
the fast-flowing Garavogue River. Thanks
to an enormous rejuvenation project,
the town centre is buzzing with shops,
cafés and trendy hotels. Sligo hosts an
annual W.B. Yeats Summer School (www.
yeatssociety.com), which celebrates its
most famous literary son. You can visit
a Yeats exhibition at the **Sligo County
Museum** (Stephen Street; www.sligo
arts.ie; Tue–Sat 9.30am–12.30pm,
May–Sept also 2–4.50pm; free). You will
find art by George Russell, Sean Keating
and Yeats's brother Jack B. Yeats, as
well as material related to the Irish rebel
and suffragette Countess Markievicz.
Another cultural highlight is **the Model,
home to the Niland Collection** (The
Mall; www.themodel.ie; Tue–Sat 10am–

Sligo on the Garavogue   *Carrowmore Megalithic Cemetery*

5pm, Sun 10.30am–3.30pm; free), with exhibitions of contemporary Irish and international art, music performances, cinema events and a strong education programme. **Lyons Café**, see ①, is a good option for breakfast.

COASTAL DRIVE

Leaving Sligo town west on the R292, you will arrive, after 5km (3 miles), at the beach resort of **Strandhill** ②. In the daytime, the town attracts families and surfers, thanks to its glorious beach and crashing waves.

For a uniquely relaxing experience, make a visit to the **Voya Seaweed Baths** (seafront; www.voyaseaweedbaths.com; daily 10am–8pm), where you can submerge yourself in a hot bath of seaweed (known for its skin-smoothing properties) or indulge in a hot-stone massage.

Knocknarea and Carrowmore

Signposted off the coast road (R292), southeast of Strandhill, is the starting-point for ascending **Knocknarea** ③, 328 metres (1,078ft) above sea level. Perched on top of the mountain is an enormous Neolithic tomb (70 by 11 metres/200 by 35ft), which is said to be the burial place of Queen Mebd (anglicised as 'Maeve'), the warrior queen of Connacht in Celtic mythology. The ascent is steep but worthwhile; the magnificent views suggest why the Celts associated this part of Ireland with myth and magic.

A little further on, just off the R292, is **Carrowmore Megalithic Cemetery** ④ (Apr–Oct 10am–6pm, last entry 5pm). Ireland's largest megalithic cemetery, it contains 6,000-year-old tombs scattered across the hillsides.

YEATS COUNTRY

Return to the R292 and continue until it meets the R287 to reach tranquil **Lough Gill** ⑤, immortalised by W.B. Yeats in the poem 'The Lake Isle of Innisfree'. Rather than driving around the Lough (a detour of some 48km/30 miles), you can stop at a viewing point, signposted just off the

Slieve League

If you have an extra day to spend in Donegal, the astonishingly beautiful cliffs of Slieve League (a transliteration of the Irish Gaelic, Sliabh Liag, meaning 'grey mountain') are a must. They are the highest marine cliffs in Europe, 650 metres (2,132ft) above sea level at their most easterly point. The cliffs are signposted from the R263 at Carrick (An Charraig). You can drive most of the way to the summit; the walk to the highest point takes in craggy towers, stunning mountain-top pools and hardy sheep. The views out towards the Atlantic, and down onto the cliffs below, are breathtaking. Another highlight is the sandy beach resort of Naran on the northern side of the peninsula (off the R261).

Lough Gill from Knocknarea

R287, by the southwest corner. Return to Sligo via the R287 and R284.

Rosses Point

If you have time, you could make a detour along the R291 (follow the signs, taking a left just past Sligo Harbour) to **Rosses Point**, with its kilometres of beautiful beach, windswept hillside walks and astonishing views both out towards the Atlantic and south towards Knocknarea. The Yeats brothers often spent long, idyllic family holidays at this pleasant spot, wistfully recounted in Yeats's writings.

Drumcliff

About 8km (5 miles) north of Sligo town, on the N15, is the churchyard of **Drumcliff ⑥**, Yeats's final resting place. Having died in France in 1939, Yeats was interred here after the Second World War. The spot is delightfully peaceful and Yeats's grave surprisingly unassuming.

MULLAGHMORE TO ROSSNOWLAGH

Signposted off the N15, 12km (7.5 miles) north of Drumcliff, is the coast road to **Mullaghmore ⑦**, with its vast swathe of golden sand and picture-postcard harbour. Before leaving Mullaghmore, follow the coastal road round to take in windswept **Mullaghmore Head**.

County Donegal beaches

Leave Mullaghmore by the road that sweeps north-east along the coast to

Yeats's grave   *Mullaghmore*

return to the N15. After 8km (5 miles) you will pass into County Donegal (via a small stretch of County Leitrim).

The first resort along the N15 is **Bundoran**, which is trying to shake off its tacky reputation. Bundoran actually marks the point at which County Donegal's 13 Blue Flag beaches begin. Between here and Donegal town, any turn off the main road will take you to one of these beaches; quiet **Rossnowlagh** is particularly recommended.

DONEGAL TOWN

Some 30km (18.5 miles) from Bundoran, following the N15 north, is lively **Donegal town** ❽, with its busy triangular 'Diamond' market square. It is a place of contrasts, as Irish-speaking locals encounter tourists in a town that, perhaps surprisingly for its northern position, contains as many familiar high-street cafés and stores as it does craft shops and tearooms. Set on the River Eske, the town is notable for its riverside **castle**, built by the O'Donnell family in the 15th century and redesigned by the Brookes, planters who took over the town in the 17th century. Donegal town is well situated for exploring the dramatic coastline of the northwestern corner of the country.

Yeats Country

Although the poet and playwright William Butler Yeats (1865–1939) was actually born in Dublin, his family moved to County Sligo soon after his birth. Yeats would come to regard the county as his ancestral and spiritual home. In 'The Lake Isle of Innisfree' Yeats drew inspiration from a small island on Lough Gill, envisaging a place where he might 'live alone in the bee-loud glade'. In one of his last poems, 'Under Ben Bulben', Yeats included a list of instructions for his burial. He was to be buried in Drumcliff churchyard, nestling under 'bare Ben Bulben's head' (referring to the mountain that dominates the Sligo coastline), and the following epitaph was to be written on his gravestone: *'Cast a cold eye/ On life, on death/ Horseman pass by!'* Yeats's requests were carried out to the letter.

Yeats's brother Jack B. Yeats (1871–1951) also derived inspiration from the area. Some of his most memorable paintings are set in and around the county.

Food and Drink

① LYONS CAFÉ

Quay Street, Sligo town; tel: 071-914 2968; www.lyonscafe.com; Mon–Sat 8.30am–6pm; €

This Sligo institution is famous for its range of home-baked goodies, especially its scones and chutneys. The lunch specials, such as lamb and pine-nut burgers with feta cheese, offer a contemporary twist.

Queen's University

BELFAST

With fewer tourists and more open spaces than Dublin, Belfast exudes a calm confidence. Impressive Victorian architecture, chic bars and restaurants, quirky museums and libraries collide in a city that buzzes with possibility.

DISTANCE: 2.5 miles (4km)
TIME: A full day
START: Botanic Gardens
END: CastleCourt Centre
TO NOTE: Buses (No 8) run from Queen's Quarter, north to Donegall Square. Buses (Metro 26 takes 20 minutes) to the Titanic Quarter depart from Wellington Place, on the northwest corner of Donegall Square, and also stop at the Albert Clock Tower. Walkers can follow the Titanic Trail signposts from the City Hall – allow 40 minutes. If you plan to take a black-taxi tour of west Belfast, it is advisable to book in the morning before you set out. Arrange for the drivers to pick you up somewhere central like Donegall Square. Belfast is very quiet on Sundays, when shops and city-centre restaurants tend to be open 1–6pm. Dublin is about 170km (105 miles) south of Belfast via the A1 and M1. Regular trains connect Belfast Central and Dublin's Connolly Station, taking 2–2.25 hours.

Belfast's dominant Victorian and Edwardian architecture resembles more a northern English city, such as Leeds or Liverpool, than the softer Georgian elegance of Dublin. But Northern Ireland's capital has other attributes. A low-rise, open city, framed between lofty green Cave Hill and the great blue bowl of Belfast Lough, it is dotted with lovely parks and open spaces and, for a major city, is surprisingly easy to get around. Above all, it's the people of Belfast who remain its great attraction. Despite preconceptions, they are among the friendliest you will meet, with an easy and down-to-earth sense of humour.

Belfast was the birthplace of the legendary *Titanic*, the most luxurious of liners built in the port's Edwardian heyday. Pride in this legacy is exemplified by the £97m visitor centre, **Titanic Belfast** in the former dockyards. The city offers a centre rich in historical and artistic legacy, with a vibrant bar and restaurant scene. A century after its golden age, Belfast has come back into its own.

Palm House in the Botanic Gardens

QUEEN'S QUARTER

Based around Victorian architect Sir Charles Lanyon's distinguished Queen's University, Queen's Quarter is an eclectic mix of elegant wine-bars, scruffy student diners, quirky bookshops and impressive architecture.

Botanic Gardens

Begin the walk at the tranquil **Botanic Gardens** ❶ (between College Park and Stranmillis Road; daily 7.30am–dusk; free), laid out in the mid-19th century. Make sure to visit Sir Charles Lanyon's restored curvilinear **Palm House**, and the **Tropical Ravine**, both of which contain exotic flora. Also within the garden is the superb **Ulster Museum** (www.nmni.com/um; Tue–Sun 10am–5pm; free), whose collection ranges from natural history to contemporary art.

Queen's University

Leave the gardens by the Stranmillis Road exit and walk north along University Road. On the right is the imposing courtyard and red-brick facade of **Queen's University** ❷, which Lanyon based on Magdalen College, Oxford. There are more than 100 listed buildings around the campus and surrounding area; to learn more you can visit the **Welcome Centre** (www.qub.ac.uk; Mon–Fri 8am–5pm; free), which also organises guided tours.

Botanic Avenue

Leave University Road by University Square, lined with Victorian terraces, to arrive at College Park, which leads to student-filled **Botanic Avenue**. Look out for shabby-chic **Café Renoir** (at no. 95), a great stop for morning coffee, see ❶, as well as the excellent crime bookshop **No Alibis** (at no. 83) and **Yellow Submarine** (at no. 44) selling vintage clothing and accessories.

SOUTH OF THE CITY CENTRE

Shaftesbury Square, at the top of Botanic Avenue, was once an integral part of Belfast's 'Golden Mile', established during the Troubles to boost the city's tourism. However, the Golden Mile has suffered from a lack of regeneration and a decline in popularity.

Ulster Hall

Leading off from the top right-hand corner of Shaftesbury Square, the Dublin Road becomes Bedford Street, home of the distinguished **Ulster Hall** (no. 34; www.ulsterhall.co.uk), a historical gem dating from 1862. It opened as a music hall, and now hosts sporting events, rock gigs, classical music concerts, and is currently home to the Ulster Orchestra. An informative display tells its history.

Great Victoria Street

Turn left beyond the Ulster Hall for Great Victoria Street. On the corner is the

Ulster Hall

glorious **Crown Liquor Saloon** ❸ (no. 46; www.nicholsonspubs.co.uk/thecrownliquorsaloonbelfast). One of the world's most beautiful Victorian pubs, it was elegantly restored by the National Trust on the advice of the poet John Betjeman. Its 10 wood-panelled snugs, which were once used by prostitutes, are now fought over by a more salubrious clientele.

Across the road is the 4-star **Europa Hotel**, which achieved the dubious fame of being 'the most bombed hotel in Europe' during the Troubles. Continue north to another ornate building. **The Grand Opera House** (www.goh.co.uk; tours Thu and Sat 11am), topped by white minarets, dates from 1895. Cross the road and turn right (east) into Wellington Place for Donegall Square.

DONEGALL SQUARE

Donegall Square, dominated by the City Hall, is the heart of the city centre. **Belfast Welcome**

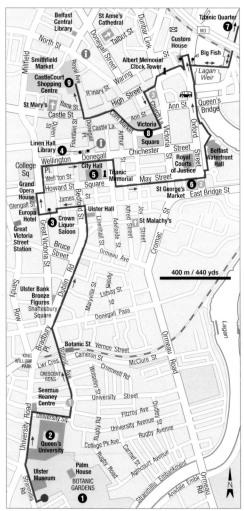

Linen Hall Library interior

City Hall

Centre (47 Donegall Place; http://visit-belfast.com; Mon–Sat 9am–5.30pm, June–Sept until 7pm, Sun 11am–4pm; free), to the north of the square, is packed full of useful information.

Linen Hall Library

On the northwestern corner of Donegall Square is the quirky **Linen Hall Library** ❹ (no. 17; www.linenhall.com; Mon–Fri 9.30am–5.30pm, Sat until 4pm; free). Belfast's oldest library, it was founded in 1788 as the Belfast Reading Society and later renamed to reflect the city's linen-producing heritage. Nowadays, it contains an intriguing selection of books and newspapers, comfortable armchairs and a small café.

City Hall

The massive **City Hall** ❺ (www.belfastcity.gov.uk; Mon–Thu 8.30am–5pm, Fri until 4.30pm, Sat–Sun 10am–4pm; tours Mon–Fri 11am, 2pm and 3pm, Sat 2pm and 3pm; free), also known as 'the stone Titanic' (the same craftsmen worked on both projects), dominates the square.

Fully renovated, this huge Renaissance Revival-style Edwardian gem, built in 1906, was inspired by London's St Paul's, and has an ornate cathedral-like interior. Even if you don't take a tour, nip in for an eyeful. The **Titanic Memorial Garden** is a favourite lunchtime spot in summer and the many monuments here include Thomas Brock's statue of Queen Victoria, and his Titanic Memorial.

WATERFRONT

Leave Donegall Square in the direction of the waterfront along May Street. After some 250 metres/yds you will find the neoclassical **Royal Courts of Justice** (1933). Facing them, on the right-hand side of the street, is **St George's Market** ❻ (www.stgeorgesmarket.com). Built in 1896 for the sale of fruit, butter, eggs and poultry, it is one of the best markets in operation in Ireland. Hugely popular and held on Fridays, Saturdays and Sundays, stalls sell a host of

---

Black cab taxi tours

An excellent way of seeing west Belfast – particularly the graphic murals of the (Catholic) Falls and (Protestant) Shankill roads and the peace line built to keep the two areas apart – is by a black-cab tour. Some cab companies are better than others and not all go to the less sanitised Shankill area, where the murals are fresher, and angrier. The tours give an invaluable insight into the political and social reality of the Troubles. A good company is Paddy Campbell's Belfast Black Cab Tours (www.belfastblackcabtours.co.uk). A one-hour 30-minute tour costs around £30 for 1–3 people (£8.50 each for 4–6 people).

Titanic's Dock and Pump House

fresh food and other goods including antiques, crafts and books. The **market stalls** offer an excellent choice for an impromptu lunch or snack, see ❷.

LAGANSIDE

Waterfront Hall

After leaving the market, turn left onto Oxford Street and right onto the pedestrianised area by the **Belfast Waterfront Hall** (2 Lanyon Place; tel: 028-9033 4455 for bookings; www.waterfront. co.uk; Mon–Sat from 10am). The glass-fronted galleries, which visitors are free to explore, afford views over Belfast and the River Lagan.

Continuing north along the riverside, pass under Sir Charles Lanyon's 1843 **Queen's Bridge**, and the modern Queen Elizabeth Bridge, to Lagan Weir. The colourful **Big Fish** sculpture has tiles depicting aspects of Belfast's history. This is the embarkation point for the *Titanic* Boat Tour (www.laganboatcompany.com).

At the northern end of Donegall Quay is the elegant mid-19th century **Custom House**, another of Lanyon's architectural achievements.

TITANIC QUARTER

To walk to the **Titanic Quarter** ❼ follow the signposts across the river. The Odyssey (www.theodyssey.co.uk) is a huge indoor arena used for basketball and rock concerts, which also houses W5 (www.w5online.co.uk), a science and discovery centre for children.

Titanic Belfast (www.titanicbelfast. com; daily Jan–Mar 10am–5pm, Apr–May, Sept 9am–6pm, June–Aug 9am–7pm, Oct–Dec 10am–5pm, last admission 1hr 40mins before closing) is an unmissable landmark, an architectural extravaganza clad in anodized aluminium, echoing the height and proportions of the gigantic ship's prow. Nine galleries on six storeys give you the

---

Giant's Causeway

If you have a day to spare, the Giant's Causeway, a 2-hour drive north of Belfast (taking the A26), is highly recommended. The existence of the Causeway – an astonishing assembly of more than 40,000 basalt columns, formed into packed hexagonal shapes by the cooling of molten lava – was not even known about until the Bishop of Derry stumbled upon it in 1692. Although the columns are relatively small – the tallest is only about 12 metres (39ft) high – the sight of them extending further out to sea, in the shadow of craggy red mountains, is breathtaking. Entrance is via the Giant's Causeway Visitor Experience (Causeway Head; www.national trust.org.uk/giants-causeway; daily July–Aug 9am–9pm, until 7pm Apr–June and Sept, until 5/6pm rest of the year), 2 miles (3km) north of Bushmills on the B146.

Titanic Belfast

Giant's Causeway

tragic story of the ship from her conception to her sinking on 14 April 1912, and its aftermath. Another site nearby associated with the Titanic is the compelling **Titanic's Dock and Pump House** (www.titanicsdock.com; Sun–Thu 10am–6pm, Fri 9.30am–6pm), where the ship stood while being fitted out.

SHOPPERS' BELFAST

Leaving the riverside area at the Custom House and heading down High Street brings you to the **Albert Memorial Clock Tower**, constructed by Queen Victoria in her husband's memory between 1865 and 1870. It leans 1.25 metres (4ft) off the vertical, rendering it Belfast's very own 'leaning tower'. About 50 metres/yds past the Clock Tower, a left turn down Church Lane, home of the excellent café-bar **Muriels**, see ③, will take you to a shopper's paradise.

The newest shopping destination, **Victoria Square** ❽ (www.victoriasquare.com; Mon, Sat 9am–6pm, Tue 9.30am–6pm, Wed–Fri 9.30am–9pm, Sun 1–6pm) has shops over four levels. The shopping streets of Ann Street, Cornmarket and Castle Street lead to Royal Avenue, home of the older, larger **CastleCourt Centre** ❾ (www.castlecourt-uk.com; Mon–Wed, Fri–Sat 9am–6pm, Thu until 9pm, Sun 1–6pm).

Food and Drink

❶ CAFÉ RENOIR
95 Botanic Avenue; tel: 028-9031 1300; Mon–Fri 8am–10pm, Sat–Sun 10am–11pm; £
This retro-style café, with a pizzeria attached, is popular with students from Queen's, thanks to its small prices and large portions. There's an excellent choice for breakfast, from pancakes to rib-eye steak, and for lunch, with options such as home-made stews and soups.

❷ ST GEORGE'S MARKET
12–20 East Bridge Street; tel: 028-9043 5704; Fri 6am–3pm, Sat 9am–3pm, Sun 10am–4pm; £

This brilliant market offers an amazing variety of lunch options. Choose from crêpes, fresh pasta, hog-roast sandwiches, home-made cakes or Chinese, Indian and Mexican food, and eat it in the central-seating area while listening to a live band.

❸ MURIEL'S
12–14 Church Lane; tel: 028-9033 2445; Mon–Fri 11.30am–1am, Sat from 10am, Sun 10am–midnight; ££

This tiny café morphs into a cocktail bar in the evening and has firmly established its reputation among Belfast's hipsters. The brunches and lunches – eggs benedict, Mexican-style sandwiches and seafood platters – are particularly popular.

DIRECTORY

Hand-picked hotels and restaurants to suit all budgets and tastes, organised by area, plus select nightlife listings, an alphabetical listing of practical information and an overview of the best books and films to give you a flavour of the city.

ACCOMMODATION

At the top end of Ireland's hotels offerings are the grand city landmarks, elegant castles and country houses. The middle range includes new hotels with elaborate spa facilities and lovingly converted period buildings. The inexpensive hotels tend to be family-owned or guest houses (just like a hotel, but with no bar or restaurant). Most B&Bs come into the economy category, but even so you can expect an en-suite bathroom and a good standard of comfort.

Book in advance June–Sept and for Dublin year round. If you are staying for more than one night, ask for a reduced rate. Book either directly with the hotel or through www.discover ireland.com, which also lists self-catering options.

Both the Irish Republic and Northern Ireland classify hotels on broadly the same grading system, as follows:

***** Top-grade hotels, some in former castles; all rooms have private bathrooms and suites are available. High-quality restaurant.

**** Hotels, ranging from modern, purpose-built premises to converted period houses, offering a high standard of comfort and service. With a few exceptions, all rooms have private bathrooms.

*** Medium-priced hotels, ranging from small, family-run places to larger, more commercial operations. Most of the rooms have private bathrooms.

** Mostly family-run hotels, with a limited but satisfactory range of food and comfort. Some rooms have private bathrooms.

* Simple but acceptable accommodation and services.

Price for a double room for one night with breakfast in the Republic of Ireland:
€€€€€ = over 200 euros
€€€€ = 160–200 euros
€€€ = 120–160 euros
€€ = 90–120 euros
€ = under 90 euros
Price for a double room for one night with breakfast in Northern Ireland:
££££ = over £200
£££ = £150–200
££ = £80–150
£ = under £80

Dublin

Aberdeen Lodge

53-55 Park Avenue; tel: 01-283 8155; www.aberdeen-lodge.com; €€€

A large three-storey Victorian house in the elegant south Dublin area of Ballsbridge, with really spacious bedrooms, all beautifully furnished. Regular buses run to the city centre, and it is also close to Sydney Parade DART station.

The Clarence, Dublin

Ariel House

50 Lansdowne Road; tel: 01-668 5512; www.ariel-house.net; €€

Elegant Victorian-style redbrick guest-house in leafy inner suburb, with a modern wing of large comfortable bedrooms. Renowned for its breakfast and the friendly welcome.

Buswell's Hotel

23–7 Molesworth Street; tel: 01-614 6500; www.buswells.ie; €€€

Georgian town houses used as a hotel since the 1920s, oozing period charm. A haunt of politicians because of its proximity to Leinster House.

Central Hotel

2 Exchequer Street; tel: 01-679 7302; www.centralhoteldublin.com; €€€

Close to both Grafton Street and Temple Bar, this rambling Victorian hotel has an excellent location, and a mildly Bohemian atmosphere. Its cosy first-floor Library Bar is a haunt of literary types.

Charles Stewart Parnell Guest House

5–6 Parnell Square; tel: 01-878 0350; www.charlesstewart.ie; €€

This lovely Georgian house is right on Parnell Square, near a bus stop to the airport. The rooms are well maintained; the young staff are helpful and enthusiastic. Excellent value.

The Clarence

6–8 Wellington Quay; tel: 01-407 0800; www.theclarence.ie; €€€€

City-centre, riverside location, backing onto Temple Bar. Refurbished and redesigned, but still retaining its keynote Art Deco panelling with stylish restraint, this place delights the eye as well as the stomach (the restaurant is first class). Owners include members of the U2 rock group and the clientele is self-consciously hip.

Clayton Hotel Ballsbridge

Merrion Road; tel: 01-668 1111; www.claytonhotelballsbridge.com; €€

A large, excellent-value hotel next to the RDS Arena, in a converted Victorian Masonic School. Over 300 rooms are offered at a flat per-room rate, with tea/coffee-making facilities. There is also a lively lounge bar and a good restaurant.

Cliff Townhouse

22 St Stephens Green; tel: 01-638 3939; www.theclifftownhouse.com; €€€€

Luxury boutique hotel above celebrated restaurant and oyster bar with a wonderful central location in Georgian Dublin; handy for shopping.

Harcourt Hotel

60 Harcourt Street; tel: 01-478 3677; www.harcourthotel.ie; €€

Harcourt occupies a row of Georgian houses just off St Stephen's Green. Rooms are small, and can be noisy as the hotel has a nightclub, but the location and ambience make it good value.

The Westbury Hotel, Dublin

The Merrion Hotel

Upper Merrion Street; tel: 01-603 0600; www.merrionhotel.com; €€€€€

A luxurious 5-star hotel, converted from four Georgian town houses, with a pool, spa and gym. Individually designed rooms and suites, each with beautiful bathrooms. So discreet it even lacks a hotel sign, using instead a small, traditional Georgian brass plaque.

Number 31

31 Lesson Close; tel: 01-676 5011; www.number31.ie; €€€€

Combining a classic Georgian town house with a Modernist 1960's mews designed by noted architect Sam Stephenson, this beautiful hotel is situated close to Fitzwilliam Square. Famous for its excellent breakfasts and unique 'sunken lounge'.

O'Callaghan Davenport

Merrion Square; tel: 01-607 3500; www.ocallaghanhotels.com; €€€€

This elegant four-star hotel is well-situated for the city centre, Merrion Square and Trinity College. Rooms are large, comfortable and surprisingly good value.

Hotel St George

7 Parnell Square; tel: 01-874 5611; www.thekeycollection.ie; €

This cosy Georgian town house has a real 'old Dublin' feel and the central location, off O'Connell Street, offers unbeatable value. The interior rooms overlooking the garden are quieter.

The Westbury Hotel

Grafton Street; tel: 01-679 1122; www.doylecollection.com; €€€€€

Consistently rated one of the most popular hotels in Dublin, the Westbury Hotel is a Dublin institution due to its 5-star luxury, its city centre location, its excellent restaurant and its afternoon tea.

Around Dublin: County Wicklow

Ashton House

Meetings of the Water, Vale of Avoca; tel: 0402-35535; www.ashtonhouseavoca. com; €

A lovely guesthouse with beautiful gardens, located right at the Meeting of the Waters. Next door to the Meetings pub for traditional Irish music sessions and a perfect pint of Guinness.

Woodenbridge Hotel & Lodge

Vale of Avoca, Arklow (on the R752); tel: 0402-35146; www.woodenbridgehotel. com; €

Established in 1608, this hotel is one of the oldest in Ireland. A bargain for County Wicklow, with bright, spacious rooms, a decent breakfast and lovely views over the Vale of Avoca. Choose the more modern Lodge to be away from the busier main hotel.

Southeast: Kilkenny

Butler House

16 Patrick Street, Kilkenny city; tel: 056-772 2828; www.butler.ie; €€

O'Callaghan Davenport hotel

Once the Dower House of Kilkenny Castle, the reception rooms here have ornate plaster ceilings and marble fireplaces, while the bedrooms have clean-lined modern decor. Breakfast is served in the Design Centre, a short walk across the garden. There's no bar or restaurant, but you are right in the centre of town. Book well in advance.

Mount Juliet Conrad
Thomastown, County Kilkenny; tel: 056-777 3000; www.mountjuliet.ie; €€€€€
This elegant 18th-century house is the centrepiece of a 600ha (1,500-acre) estate by the River Nore, which includes a Jack Nicklaus-designed golf course, equestrian centre, fishing, archery, falconry, tennis and luxury spa. Rooms in the main house have impeccable period decor plus modern facilities, albeit at a price. For less formal dining, Kendal's is a French brasserie which ticks all the boxes.

Zuni Townhouse
26 Patrick Street, Kilkenny city; tel: 056-772 3999; www.zuni.ie; €
Town-centre boutique hotel with minimalist decor, free parking, chic cocktail bar and a popular restaurant serving modern Irish food with influences from around the globe.

Southeast: Waterford & Cashel

Bailey's Hotel Cashel
42 Main Street, Cashel; tel: 062-6715147; www.baileyshotelcashel.com; €€

A sympathetically restored Georgian building in the centre of Cashel. Free entry into the Rock of Cashel with every booking. Comfortable surroundings with underfloor heating.

Dooley's Hotel
The Quay, Waterford city; tel: 051-873 531; www.dooleys-hotel.ie; €€
Family-run hotel with good food and lively bar in centre of town on the River Suir.

Granville Hotel
The Quay, Waterford city; tel: 051-305 555; www.granville-hotel.ie; €€
The Granville's porticoed entrance has been a landmark on Waterford's quays for generations. The hotel has retained its Georgian character through many refurbishments, but remains likeably old fashioned. It is perfectly located for exploring the city on foot.

Southwest: Cork city and environs

Ballymaloe House
Shanagarry, Midleton; tel: 021-465 2531; www.ballymaloe.ie; €€€€€
One of Ireland's leading country house hotels and one of the world's leading cookery schools, Ballymaloe is set in a beautiful part of East Cork. The kitchen is renowned for its pioneering use of fresh local produce, including home-grown vegetables and ripe fruit from the hotel's own farm. It is less

Mount Juliet Conrad grounds

than an hour's drive east of Cork city off the N25.

Clayton Hotel Cork City
Lapp's Quay, Cork; tel: 021-422 4900; www.claytonhotelcorkcity.com; €€

A large hotel in the centre of town by the River Lee, the Clayton is a pioneer of the proposed docklands development. There's a central atrium with a wide staircase, which some bedrooms overlook; if you want an exterior view, say so. Bedrooms have chic, minimalist decor, while the bar extends on to a riverside walk and is a popular early evening spot.

Gabriel House
Summerhill North, St Luke's Cross, Cork; tel: 021-450 0333; www.gabriel-house. ie; €

This large detached building was previously a Christian Brothers seminary, but now makes a characterful budget hotel from which to explore the city. It's on a bluff high above the railway station, a five-minute walk uphill from the centre; the best and largest rooms have a river view.

Hotel Isaacs
48 MacCurtain Street, Cork; tel: 021-450 0011; www.isaacscork.com; €

Charming Victorian hotel with contemporary interior tucked away under an archway off a busy road. Handy for both bus and train stations.

Old Presbytery
43 Cork Street, Kinsale; tel: 021-477 2027; www.oldpres.com; €€€

Characterful old town house furnished with an attractive medley of antiques and offering a high standard of comfort. There is self-catering accommodation available in an annexe to the main building. Quiet town-centre location.

Rolf's Country House
Baltimore Hill, Baltimore; tel: 028-20289; www.rolfscountryhouse.com; €€€€

A converted old stone-built farmhouse and outbuildings on a site high above Roaring Water Bay. Bedrooms are small and simple, with white cotton bedlinen and casement windows, and there are self-catering cottages available. The restaurant is pleasantly informal, with exhibitions by local artists. The village is about 1.5km (1 mile) away and has a lively pub and café scene in summer.

Trident Hotel
Kinsale; tel: 021-477 9300; www.tridenthotel.com; €€

Watch the boats come and go from this modern waterside hotel, adjacent to the town pier, where all rooms have sea views. The Wharf Tavern is popular with locals for bar food.

Butler Arms Hotel
Waterville; tel: 066-947 4144; www.butlerarms.com; €€€

Limerick and the Shannon at dusk

Well-established, informal hotel overlooking the sea that has been run by the same family since 1916. Golf, tennis, shooting, fishing. The cast and crew of Star Wars stayed here when filming *The Force Awakens* in 2014 and 2015.

Carrig Country House

Caragh Lake, Glenbeigh; tel: 066-976 9100; www.carrighouse.com; €€€€

You can hear the waters of the lake lapping from your bedroom in this magical hideaway. The Victorian manor house is set in carefully tended lakeside gardens, with views of the wild mountains. Bedrooms are furnished in Victorian style with antique furniture; the peaceful sitting room is lined with books; and the restaurant is excellent.

Loch Lein Country House Hotel

Fossa, Killarney; tel: 064-663 1260; www.lochlein.com; €€€

Situated 4km (2.5 miles) outside Killarney just off the main Ring of Kerry (N72), this 25-room hotel makes an excellent touring base. It occupies a secluded location with tantalising views of Loch Lein across the fields.

Parknasilla Resort

Sneem; tel: 064-667 5600; www.parknasillaresort.com; €€€€

Set amid 200ha (500 acres) of balmy sub-tropical vegetation on a sheltered sea inlet, with a dramatic backdrop of mountains, this is one of Ireland's most famous resort hotels. Opt for a room in the main house or the less expensive self-catering lodges (two bedrooms) and villas (three bedrooms). The bedrooms have been fully upgraded, as have the pool and spa, while the lounge and bar retain a mildly eccentric old-fashioned charm.

Sea Lodge Waterville

Waterville; tel: 066-947 8533; www.sealodgewaterville.ie; €€€

Luxurious, modern boutique hotel with a nautical theme. Stunning views across Ballinskelligs Bay. The village of Waterville was Charlie Chaplin's favourite holiday destination and the village hosts an annual Charlie Chaplin festival.

Southwest: Dingle Peninsula/Tralee

Ballygarry House Hotel and Spa

Killarney Road, Tralee; tel: 066 712 3322; www.ballygarryhouse.com; €€€

This family-run country house-style hotel has been extended without losing the quiet charm of the original. 2.5km (1.5 miles) outside town, it is a great touring base, with mountain views, and forest walking trails on the doorstep. The bar has a large local clientele, and the restaurant is a favourite for special occasions, while residents can enjoy their own drawing room and library. The spa is excellent.

Dromoland Castle, County Clare

Dingle Skellig Hotel

Dingle; tel: 066-915 0200; www.dingle
skellig.com; €€€
Well-designed modern hotel on the
water's edge. Sea view on request.
Indoor pool and spa. Renowned for its
family-friendly ethos.

Greenmount House

Upper John Street, Dingle; tel: 066-915
1414; www.greenmounthouse.ie; €€€
Although only a short walk from the
town centre, this quiet 14-room guesthouse is surrounded by country fields
and has a lovely view of the sun setting
over Dingle Harbour. Rooms are spacious, with uncluttered contemporary
decor. The home-baking and breakfast
here are famed.

West: Limerick and Shannon

Dromoland Castle

Newmarket-on-Fergus, County Clare; tel:
061-368 144; www.dromoland.ie. €€€€€
If you can only sample one luxury
castle hotel, choose this one. Once
the ancestral home of the O'Briens,
direct descendants of Brian Ború who
defeated the Vikings in 1014, the baro-
nial-style hotel has splendid views over
the lake and golf course. Even though
the public rooms are awe-inspiringly
grand, staff are so friendly that guests
quickly feel at home.

Dunraven Arms Hotel

Adare, County Limerick; tel: 061-605 900;
www.dunravenhotel.com; €€€

Beautifully refurbished historic inn in
picture-book pretty village. Equestrian
and golf holidays are a speciality.

Fitzgerald's Woodlands House Hotel

Knockanes, Adare, County Limerick; tel:
061-605 100; www.woodlands-hotel.ie; €€
This unpretentious, friendly family-run
hotel about 1.5km (1 mile) outside
Adare is a good touring base, within
easy reach of Shannon Airport. It has a
lively bistro and a more formal restaurant. Constant additions and refurbishment have also given it a pool, a large
gym and an above-average spa.

West: the Cliffs of Moher and the Burren

Gregan's Castle

Ballyvaughan, County Clare; tel: 065-707
7005; www.gregans.ie; €€€€€
This is one of Ireland's finest country
house hotels, a quiet retreat at the base
of the Burren's famous Corkscrew Hill,
with breathtaking views over Galway Bay.
The elegant decor features fine antiques
and contemporary Irish art. A warm welcome and a renowned restaurant make it
a favourite hideaway. Be warned, there is
only one TV in the house.

Hyland's Burren Hotel

Ballyvaughan, County Clare; tel: 065-707
7037; www.hylandsburren.com; €€
Hyland's is a typical, much-extended
19th-century village-centre hotel with
a restaurant and lively bar. Most rooms

Dunraven Arms Hotel, Adare

have glorious views of the surrounding limestone hills.

The G

Wellpark; tel: 091-865 200; www.theghotel.ie; €€€€

Dedicated followers of fashion will not mind paying a premium to experience a wildly different hotel with an extravagant sense of fun and great art on the walls. Designed by hat-maker extraordinaire Philip Treacy, the colourful reception rooms contrast with the soothingly tranquil bedrooms. It also has a seriously good spa.

Glenlo Abbey Hotel

Bushy Park; tel: 091-526 666; www.glenloabbeyhotel.ie; €€€€

Luxuriously converted monastery on the banks of Lough Corrib, 4km (2.5 miles) west of the city centre, surrounded by its own golf course. Other activities include yoga, falconry and fishing. Treat yourself to afternoon tea aboard a 1940's train carriage in the Pullman Restaurant.

Grand Hotel Meyrick

Eyre Square; tel: 091-564 041; www.hotelmeyrick.ie; €€€

Grand old railway hotel on city's main square, formerly the Galway Great Southern; still a major landmark and social centre.

The House Hotel

Spanish Parade; tel: 091-538 900; www.thehousehotel.ie; €€€

A stylish boutique hotel with a prime location in Galway's Latin Quarter, the House will make a memorable – and convenient – base in the centre of the shopping and pubbing district. Bedrooms in this warehouse conversion are compact but comfortable, with snazzy contemporary decor. The real star here is the House Cocktail Bar (with live music at weekends).

Park House Hotel

Forster Street, Eyre Square; tel: 091-564 924; www.parkhousehotel.ie; €€€

An old stone warehouse has been converted and extended to create a welcoming hotel. Bedrooms have warm decor and are sufficiently glazed to mute noisy Galway nightlife. Right in the city centre, the bar and lobby area are favourites with locals.

Abbeyglen Castle Hotel

Sky Road, Clifden, County Galway; tel: 095-21201; www.abbeyglen.ie; €€€€

A delightfully old-fashioned manor house hotel, superbly located on a height above Clifden Bay in extensive gardens and a short walk from town, this is an ideal base for touring Connemara. The room price includes afternoon tea, a great rainy day treat. Rooms vary in size and aspect; the best ones are in the front of the house, but all have an old-world charm. At night the bar and restaurant are lively spots.

Ardagh Hotel

Ballyconneely Road, Clifden, County Galway; tel: 095-21384; www.ardaghhotel.com; €€€

Quiet family-run hotel 2km (1.2 miles) from Clifden on Ardbear Bay. Excellent restaurant specialising in seafood.

Ashford Castle

Cong, County Mayo; tel: 094-954 6003; www.ashford.ie; €€€€€

A fairy-tale castle, standing between loughs Corrib and Mask, Ashford never fails to impress. American-owned, it has very high standards of comfort and decor, a private golf course, tennis, fishing, boating, horse riding, falconry, shooting and extensive gardens.

West: Westport town

Knockranny House Hotel

Castlebar Road, Westport; tel: 098-28600; www.knockrannyhousehotel.ie; €€€

Large, luxurious hotel on the edge of town with splendid views of Croagh Patrick, an excellent restaurant and award-winning spa.

Westport Plaza, Westport Coast and Castlecourt Hotel

Castlebar Street, Westport town; tel: 098-55088; www.westporthotelgroup.ie; €€€

These sister-hotels in the centre of Westport are run by the same family, and share a leisure centre and spa, but have separate identities. The less expensive Castlecourt is a comfortable, traditional hotel catering for holiday and business clients, while the more chic (and expensive) Plaza is a boutique-style hotel with Chesterfield sofas in its reception area and pleasantly luxurious bedrooms. The Coast is the only waterfront hotel in Westport and has stunning views over Clew Bay.

Northwest: Sligo town

Great Southern Hotel Sligo

Strandhill Road; tel: 071-916 2101; www.greatsouthernhotelsligo.ie; €€

A 'superior' 3-star hotel, right in the centre of town, with its own leisure centre, orient express bar with live music on Saturday nights and garden room restaurant. Although the interior is a little faded, the hotel is excellent value; consider upgrading to a suite for great views and a private jacuzzi.

Sligo Park Hotel

Pearse Road; tel: 071-919 0400; www.sligoparkhotel.com; €€

Scenic location 1.5km (1 mile) south of town with gardens and leisure centre. Appeals to families with great-value packages.

Northwest: Donegal town

Ard na Breatha Guesthouse

Drumrooske Middle; tel: 074-972 2200; www.ardnabreatha.com; €€

An award-winning guesthouse 2km (1.25 miles) outside Donegal town. The bedrooms are bright and spacious. Breakfast choices include the 'full Irish', smoked salmon and pancakes. Highly recommended.

Ashford Castle, County Mayo

Harvey's Point Country Hotel

Lough Eske; tel: 074-972 2208;
www.harveyspoint.com; €€€€

Modern luxurious lakeside complex with sports facilities. The award-winning restaurant is a huge draw, as are the well-appointed rooms.

Mill Park

The Mullins; tel: 074-972 2880;
www.millparkhotel.com; €€€

A large hotel close to Donegal town, with a choice of rooms and suites, a leisure centre (including pool, sauna and steam room) and a restaurant specialising in seafood.

Northern Ireland: Belfast

Benedicts Hotel

7–21 Bradbury Place; tel: 028-9059 1999;
www.benedictshotel.co.uk; ££

Good value boutique-style hotel with an excellent restaurant, which uses local produce.

Madison's

59–63 Botanic Avenue; tel: 028-9050 9800;
www.madisonshotel.com; ££

A stylish bar, a trendy nightclub, a popular bistro and elegant rooms are the star attractions here in the leafy environs of Queen's University.

The Merchant Hotel

16 Skipper Street; tel: 028-9023 4888;
www.themerchanthotel.com; ££££

The former headquarters of Ulster Bank has been exuberantly converted into a luxury hotel while retaining many of the original architectural features. Since opening in 2006 in the arty Cathedral Quarter, this hotel has come to epitomise Belfast's new identity as a hot destination. The huge former banking hall is now the breathtakingly grand Great Room Restaurant.

Tara Lodge

36 Cromwell Road; tel: 028-9059 0900; www.taralodge.com; ££

Well located just off Botanic Avenue, Tara Lodge combines the facilities of a hotel with the friendliness of a guesthouse. The rooms are spacious and comfortable and the staff helpful.

Ten Square Hotel

10 Donegall Square South; tel: 028-9024 1001; www.tensquare.co.uk; £££

A listed Victorian linen warehouse has been transformed into an ultra-luxurious hotel with oriental decor and an emphasis on style. Right in the centre of town at Donegall Square.

Youth Hostels

The Irish Youth Hostel Association, An Óige, has a comprehensive website (www.anoige.ie) with an excellent choice of hostels throughout the Republic. For hostels in Northern Ireland, Hostelling International NI (www.hini.org.uk) has hostels in Belfast and on the Causeway coast.

Temple Bar, Dublin

RESTAURANTS

After years in the gastronomic wilderness, Ireland has embraced modern cooking with great enthusiasm. Some of the best restaurants in the country are still to be found in hotels, but they are a far cry from the days of overcooked meat and soggy vegetables. Now, a light-handed approach allows the natural flavours of fresh local produce to shine through. Nowhere in Ireland is more than a two-hour drive from the sea, and fresh seafood is a much-prized ingredient. The Irish dining scene is consistently informal: even the grandest hotels specify 'smart but casual', meaning a jacket for men, but no obligatory tie. Advance booking is advisable at weekends and in summer.

While the cities have a wide range of small restaurants, in the countryside pubs are a major element in the eating-out scene. Many are now more like restaurants than the drinking dens of yore, and most welcome children during daylight hours. And thanks to the smoking ban, outdoor tables are commonplace; all you need is the weather to enjoy them.

Dublin

777

7 Castle House, South Great George's Street; tel: 01-425 4052; www.777.ie; Mon–Wed 5.30–10pm, Thu until 11pm, Fri–Sat until midnight, Sun 2–10pm; €€

Fun Mexican restaurant with bold flavours and vibrant colours, offering Dublin's largest selection of tequilas. Famous for their Margaritas, and the tapas-style menu with dishes to share at €7.77.

Ananda

Sandyford Road, Dundrum Town Centre; tel: 01-296 0099; www.anandarestaurant. io; Mon–Sat 5.30–10.45pm, also Fri–Sat 12.30–2.30pm, Sun 1–2.45pm, 5.30–9.30pm; €€€€

This restaurant from Atul Kochhar, chef-patron of the Michelin-starred Indian restaurant Benares in London, opened in 2008. The intricate presentation and delicate spicing of the dishes – a wonderful *amuse-bouche* of lentil soup, a

<table>
<tr><td>Price guide for a two-course dinner for one in the Republic of Ireland:
€€€€ = over 40 euros
€€€ – 30–40 euros
€€ = 20–30 euros
€ = under 20 euros
Price guide for a two-course dinner for one in Northern Ireland:
££££ = over £40
£££ = £25–40
££ = £15–25
£ = under £15</td></tr>
</table>

Hugo's Restaurant and Wine Bar

divine crab terrine and fabulous thalis – will blow you away. Excellent-value early-bird dinners from 5.30–6.30pm.

Café en Seine

40 Dawson Street; tel: 01-677 4567; www.cafeenseine.ie; food served daily noon–9pm, Sun until 5pm; €€

Stunning Art Deco interior with three-storey atrium featuring intimate bars within bars. It's the trendy place to be. The casual, contemporary food is on offer all day and well into the night.

Chapter One

18–19 Parnell Square; tel: 01-873 2266; www.chapteronerestaurant.com; Tue–Sat 5.30–10.30pm, also Tue–Fri 12.30–2pm; €€€€

Michelin-starred. One of Dublin's leading restaurants, it has a well-deserved reputation for superb, friendly service and outstanding classic/modern Irish cooking that showcases specialist Irish produce. A highlight is the Chef's Table, in particular the six-course menu. A meal here is a special treat (reserve well in advance). Lunch, and their renowned pre-theatre menu (dessert served after the theatre show), are great value.

Chez Max

1 Palace Street; tel: 01-633 7215; www.chezmax.ie; Sun–Thu 5.30–10pm, Fri–Sat until11pm, also Sun–Fri noon–3.30pm, Sat noon–4pm; €€

Classic French dishes at exceptionally reasonable prices for the high quality of food, cooking and table service.

Cornucopia

19–20 Wicklow Street; tel: 01-677 7583; www.cornucopia.ie; Mon 8.30am–9pm, Tue–Sat until 10pm, Sun noon–9pm; €

Generations of Trinity students have refuelled at this vegetarian and vegan-friendly wholefood restaurant where the generous portions of tasty fare recall the best home-cooking. Excellent breakfast.

Dunne & Crescenzi

14–16 South Frederick Street; tel: 01-675 9892; www.dunneandcrescenzi.com; Mon–Sat 8am–11pm, Sun 9.30am–10pm; €€

Billed as an authentic *'enoteca Italiana'*, this Italian restaurant and deli is renowned for its simple food and good wine. The prosciutto and mozzarella bars are a particular treat.

L'Ecrivain

109a Lower Baggot Street; tel: 01-661 1919; www.lecrivain.com; Mon–Sat 6.30–10.30pm, also Thu–Fri 12.30–2pm; €€€€

Michelin star. An exceptional place in every way. Chef/patron Derry Clarke and his gifted team have a unique cooking style based on classic French with contemporary flair and a strong leaning towards contemporary Irish cooking using carefully sourced ingredients from artisan producers.

Eden Restaurant, Dublin

Eden Restaurant

7 South William Street; tel: 01-670 6887; www.edenbarandgrill.ie; daily noon–4pm, 5.30–10pm; €€€

Simple, light Irish cooking that reflects the flavours and products of the countryside, farms and seas of Ireland.

Ely Wine Bar

22 Ely Place; tel: 01-676 8986; www.elywinebar.ie; Mon–Fri noon–11.30pm, Sat 5pm–12.30am; €€€

Just off St Stephen's Green, this Georgian townhouse recalls the gracious Dublin of old. The list of more than 400 wines, many by the glass, is renowned. Traditional fare, including rare-breed pork sausages, steaks of organic and dry-aged beef, is largely sourced on the family farm in County Clare, while seafood is fresh from the Atlantic. A much bigger and contemporary Ely gastropub and a brasserie (see website) are in the same family.

Market Bar

Fade Street; tel: 01-613 9094; www.marketbar.ie; food served Mon–Thu noon–11.30pm, Fri–Sat until 1.30am, Sun until 11pm; €€

A gorgeous cavernous bar serving an exciting selection of tapas – Cajun sea trout, steamed mussels, beef stew – in small or large portions, with a good choice of wine.

Yamamori Noodles

71–72 South Great George's Street; tel: 01-475 5001; www.yamamorinoodles.ie; Sun–Thu noon–10.30pm, Fri–Sat until 11.30pm; €€

A popular Japanese restaurant serving freshly prepared noodles, sushi and ramen. Try the clay seafood hotpot or the good-value daily bento-box specials.

Around Dublin: County Wicklow

The Happy Pear

Church Road, Greystones; tel: 01-287 3655; www.thehappypear.ie; Mon–Thu 9am–6pm, Fri–Sun until 8pm; €€€

Located in a seaside village (beside the DART rail station) this is the home of the phenomenally successful and internationally renowned Happy Pear vegetarian café and veg shop.

Roundwood Inn

Roundwood (N11); tel: 01-281 8107; bar menu daily noon–8.45pm, restaurant Fri–Sat 7.30–9pm, Sun 1–2pm; €€€

Situated in Wicklow's highest village, en route to Glendalough, this 17th-century inn serves Irish-German fusion cuisine, with an emphasis on locally sourced meat and fish for dishes such as crab bisque, Wicklow trout, suckling pig and, in winter, roasted stuffed goose.

Southeast: County Kilkenny

Footlights By The River

The Square, Inistioge; tel: 086-361 9411; www.footlights.ie; daily noon–8pm, Fri–Sat until 10pm, Nov–Mar Sat and Sun only; €€

The decor is stylishly contemporary at this child-friendly bistro in a period riverside house. Snacks include ciabattas, salads and pizzas, while mains are prepared using fresh, locally sourced produce. BYOB service with no corkage.

Southeast: County Wexford

Beaches Restaurant and La Marine Bistro

Kelly's Resort Hotel, Rosslare; tel: 053-913 2114; www.kellys.ie; Beaches 1–2pm, 7.30–9pm, €€€; La Marine 12.30–2.15pm, 6.30–9pm, €€

Family-run for more than 100 years, Beaches is formal fine dining and provides classic cooking. Menus change daily. La Marine offers relaxed, contemporary European-style menus with the odd Asian spin.

Harvest Room Restaurant

Dunbrody Country House Hotel, Arthurstown, New Ross; tel: 051 389600; www.dunbrodyhouse.com; daily 6.30–9.15pm, also Sun 1.30–3pm; €€€€

Talented TV chef Kevin Dundon serves some of Irish cuisine's most spectacular food at this small luxury hotel. The emphasis is on simple but imaginative combinations of fresh ingredients. The elaborate desserts are legendary. There is also a more informal Champagne & Seafood Bar (Mon–Sat 2–10pm, Sun 3.30–10pm; €€) with a choice of 16 items in starter-size portions.

Southeast: County Waterford

La Bohème

2 George's Street, Waterford; tel: 051-875 645; www.labohemerestaurant.ie; Mon–Sat 5.30–11.30pm, Sun until 10.30pm, also Fri 12.30–2.30pm; €€€€

Run with style by owner/chef Eric Theze. A serious restaurant, French style all the way. Expensive, but worth it. Closes annually in January.

The Tannery

10 Quay Street, Dungarvan; tel: 058-45420; www.tannery.ie; Tue–Sat 5.30–9pm, Sun 6–9pm, also Fri 12.30–2.30pm and Sun 12.30–4pm; €€€

An old stone warehouse has been converted into a minimalist first-floor restaurant. Owner-chef Paul Flynn's cooking attracts food lovers from miles away. Start with crab crème brulée with pickled cucumber, followed by slow-cooked ox cheek. Closes annually for the last two weeks of January.

Southwest: Cork city

Café Paradiso

16 Lancaster Quay, Western Road; tel: 021-427 7939; www.cafeparadiso.ie; Mon–Sat 5.30–10pm; €€

Owner-cook Denis Cotter has transformed the reputation of vegetarian cooking at his small but stylish restaurant. Even carnivores look forward to his imaginative, robustly spiced combinations of seasonal fare: in

summer, perhaps, eggroll pancake of asparagus and Coolea cheese with a warm cherry tomato and fennel salsa; in autumn the signature pumpkin risotto.

Cornstore

40A Cornmarket Street; tel: 021-427 4777; www.cornstorecork.com; daily noon–4pm, 5–10.30pm; €€€

A granite warehouse conversion in Cork's open-air market district over two floors, this is a buzzy dining experience in a Manhattan-style setting. Seafood is a speciality, as are their premium steaks, which include a Chateaubriand (fillet carved for two).

Greenes

48 MacCurtain Street; 021-455 2279; www.greenesrestaurant.com; Sun–Tue, Thu–Sat 12.15–2.15pm, 5.30-9.00pm, Wed 12.15–2.30pm, 5.30–9pm; €€

Turn off busy MacCurtain Street into a small cobblestoned alley for a pleasant surprise: at night this Victorian warehouse conversion is floodlit and a natural waterfall runs down one wall; by day there are outdoor tables. Seafood is the speciality here, but meat and vegetarian food is also offered in Mediterranean-style dishes and Asian-influenced fusion cuisine.

Isaacs Restaurant

48 MacCurtain Street; tel: 021-450 3805; www.isaacsrestaurant.ie; Mon–Sat 12.30–2.30pm, 5.30–10pm, Sun 6–9pm; €€

Spacious converted warehouse. Relaxed, fun and vibrant. Good service, quality ingredients, and consistently excellent cooking delivered at a fair price. The food style is a mix of international and traditional, with good vegetarian options.

Jacob's Ladder

Water's Edge Hotel, Cobh; tel: 021-481 5566; www.watersedgehotel.ie; daily noon–9pm; €€

Jacob's Ladder is a minimalist, contemporary bar-restaurant featuring a mesmerising panoramic harbour view. This is complemented by a varied and imaginative menu with an Irish accent: baked ham with parsley sauce, for example. It's also a great place to come for a coffee or a cocktail.

Southwest: West Cork coast

Fishy Fishy Restaurant

Crowley's Pier, Kinsale; tel: 021-470 0415; www.fishyfishy.ie; daily noon–9pm, Sun–Wed until 4pm in winter; €€€

One of Ireland's leading seafood restaurants occupies two floors of a substantial house in the town park. If you have never tried real scampi made from freshly caught prawns, do so here. The salads are huge, with the warm seafood salad a lunchtime favourite.

Mary Ann's

Castletownshend, Skibbereen; tel: 028-36146; daily noon–2.30pm,

6–9pm, Nov–Mar closed Mon; bar €, restaurant €€€

Said to be one of the oldest bars in Ireland, this dream gastropub is hidden away in a picturesque fishing village. Packed in summer, with a large patio, it's even more charming in winter, when there might be only a few diners in the low-ceilinged bar. Daily specials include hot crab gratin or lobster thermidor, while the seafood platter is legendary.

Southwest: the Ring of Kerry

The Park Hotel

Kenmare; tel: 064-664 1200; www.parkkenmare.com; daily lounge 11am–6pm, dining room noon–3pm, 7–9pm; €€€€

Kenmare is the foodie capital of southwest Ireland and the Park is the jewel in its crown. The elegant dining room, built in 1897 by the Great Southern Railway, is imposing but friendly. Food is light but flavoursome, featuring seafood and local specialities, such as Kerry lamb and Skeaghanore West Cork duck. The bar and lounge serve a lighter menu during the day.

QC's

Church Street, Cahirciveen; tel: 066-947 2244; www.qcbar.com; Mon–Sat 12.30–11.30pm, Sun 6–9.30pm (with exceptions in winter); €€€

A culinary highlight of Kerry, this award-winning seafood restaurant serves fish from its own fleet of trawlers, and local game in season. At the western end of town on the main (N70) road.

Southwest: the Dingle Peninsula

Ashe's Bar

Main Street, Dingle; tel: 066-915 0989; www.ashesbar.ie; food served daily noon–3pm, 5.30–9.30pm; €€

Ashe's pioneered bar food locally, feeding the cast of *Ryan's Daughter* in 1969. The pub is cosy, quirky and old fashioned, but the menu is bang up to date, with prawn tempura, oysters, rib eye steak and squid salad.

The Chart House

The Mall, Dingle; tel: 066-915 2255; www.thecharthousedingle.com; daily from 6pm, restricted opening off-season, phone to confirm; €€

The bright red half-door of Jim McCarthy's stone-built cottage restaurant is the first thing you see on arriving at Dingle. A favourite starter is local black pudding in filo pastry with apple and date chutney and hollandaise sauce. Pork is served with brandied apples, pan-fried brill with smoked bacon and rocket. Desserts are a highlight.

West: Limerick city & Shannon

Maguire Restaurant

At the Dunraven Arms, Adare; tel: 061-605 900; www.dunravenhotel.com; daily 7.30–9.30pm, also Sun 12.30–1.30pm; €€€

Country house atmosphere and a menu that offers genuine traditional dishes. A big draw is real roast rib of beef carved at the table.

Sash Restaurant

1 Pery Square, Limerick; tel: 061-402 402; www.oneperysquare.com; Mon–Fri 7.15–10am, Tue–Thu 5.30–9pm, Fri–Sat until 9.30pm, also Sat–Sun 8.30–11am, Sat 1pm–3pm and Sun 1–6pm; €€

This elegant hotel in a Georgian town house is close to the city centre overlooking the People's Park. The classy but informal Sash Restaurant is on the first floor and serves breakfast, lunch and dinner in cosy, convivial surroundings.

The Wild Geese

Rose Cottage, Main Street, Adare; tel: 061-396451; www.thewild-geese.com; Tue–Sat from 6.30pm, Sun 12.30–2pm; €€€

Located in one of Adare's thatched cottages, this is a serious restaurant, with a well-travelled owner-chef offering excellent modern Irish cuisine. The menu makes use of a wide choice of top-quality ingredients. Seared scallops and chorizo are served on buttered leeks, while marinated loin of venison comes with savoy cabbage and parsnip purée.

West: the Cliffs of Moher and the Burren

Moran's Oyster Cottage

The Weir, Kilcolgan; tel: 091-796113; www.moransoystercottage.com; Mon–Thu noon–11.30pm, Fri–Sat until midnight, Sun until 11pm; €€

One of the quintessential west of Ireland experiences is a seafood feast at Moran's. The tiny thatched pub is 500 metres/yds off the N18 (signposted in Kilcolgan), beside a wide weir and the Moran family's oyster beds. The front bar has been preserved, but there is also a large restaurant behind. Local oysters are in season from September to April; in summer there's crab and lobster.

The Pier Head

The Quay, Kinvara; tel: 091-638188; www.pierhead.ie; food served Mon–Sat noon–10pm, Sun until 9.30pm; €€

A corner bar on The Quay, with plate-glass windows offering views of Dunguaire Castle and the evening sunset across the bay, which is hugely popular locally. Sample the excellent seafood – mussels, skate and lobster – and locally sourced steak on the short but impeccably prepared menu.

West: Galway city

Ard Bia Café

By Spanish Arch; tel: 091-561114; www.ardbia.com; café daily 10am–3.30pm, restaurant daily 6–10pm; €€

This compact waterside stone warehouse, with bare wooden floors and quirky art on the walls, is an atmospheric spot for a casual meal, featuring local artisan food. Pricier meals are served in the upstairs restaurant in the evening.

A healthy beef dish

The Kings Head Bistro

15 High Street; tel: 091-566630;
www.thekingshead.ie; Mon–Sat 10.30am–
10pm, Sun 11.30am–10pm; €€

Previously the Malthouse, the Kings
Head Bistro is connected to the pub of
the same name. Perfect for a casual
bite to eat in a relaxed atmosphere,
right in the centre of Galway.

The Seafood Bar @ Kirwan's

Kirwan's Lane; tel: 091-568266;
www.kirwanslane.com; Mon–Sun 6–10pm,
also Mon–Sat 12.30–2.30pm; €€€

Kirwan's Lane is a quiet medieval alleyway off Galway's long main street, and
the restaurant is a smart, contemporary
space on two airy levels. The cuisine is
contemporary Irish, specialising in seafood but with plenty of choice from meat
to vegetarian dishes.

Viña Mara

19 Middle Street; tel: 091-561610;
www.vinamara.com; Mon–Fri 12.30–
2.30pm, 6–10pm, Sat 12.30–3pm,
5.30–10pm; €€

This former shop is now an intimate
restaurant serving food, sourced
locally when possible. Among the
chef's specialities is potted salmon
with seaweed butter, and slow-cooked
Irish beef.

West: Connemara

Leenane Hotel

Leenane, Co Mayo; tel: 095-42249;
www.leenanehotel.com; bar daily noon–
6pm, €; restaurant daily 6.30–9pm, closed
mid-Nov–Easter; €€

This venerable old hotel overlooking
Killary Fjord serves bar food beside the
open fire at lunchtime. In the evening
the dining room is packed with savvy
punters tucking into a great-value
menu. This includes baked Killary Bay
salmon with lime *beurre blanc*, and
rack of Connemara mountain lamb.

The Owenmore Restaurant

Ballynahinch Castle Hotel, Recess, Co.
Galway; tel: 095-31006; www.ballynahinch-
castle.com; bar daily noon–6pm, €€;
restaurant daily 6.30–9pm, €€€€

It's not really a castle but a massive Victorian mansion with crenellations, set in
romantic woodland on the Ballynahinch
River. The five-course set dinner menu
offers a wide choice of classic dishes,
including local game. Meals are also
served in the bar.

West: Westport town

La Fougère

Knockranny House Hotel and Spa; tel: 098-
28600; www.khh.ie; daily 6–9pm; €€€€

This Victorian-style hotel was built on
an elevated site overlooking the town.
The hotel dining room, La Fougère
(The Fern) has views across the town
to Croagh Patrick and Clew Bay, and
creates a sense of occasion with its
traditional table settings. The menus
offer a wide choice of fine local produce, including Mayo mountain lamb
and Clare Island salmon.

Hargadon's Pub, Sligo town

Northwest: Sligo town

Hargadon's Bar

4–5 O'Connell Street; tel: 071-915 3709; www.hargadons.com; food served Mon–Sat noon–9pm; €

One of Ireland's great traditional pubs, its interior has changed very little since its opening back in 1864. The restaurant serves a simple menu of hearty fare, much of it organic and locally produced – from oysters to crab linguini, bangers and mash and the farmhouse cheese platter – at great prices.

Montmartre

1 Market Yard; tel: 071-916 9901; www.mont martrerestaurant.ie; Tue–Sat 5–11pm; €€

Montmartre's owner/chef is French and pleases locals and homesick French visitors alike. Children welcome.

The Venue

Strandhill; tel: 071-916 8167; www.venue strandhill.ie; daily 12.30–9pm; €€

Traditional and friendly, the Venue serves top-notch steak and seafood. Try the Lissadell mussels, crab claws and seafood chowder.

Northwest: Donegal town

Ard Na Breatha Restaurant

Drumrooske Middle, Donegal Town; tel: 074-972 2288; www.ardnabreatha.com; daily 7–9.30pm; reservations essential; €€€

Organic, locally sourced seasonal food served in pleasant, bright surroundings. The three-course set menu is standard, but you can just have one or

two courses. The Irish cheeseboard is a must. There's also a snug bar with a roaring fire.

Olde Castle Bar and Red Hugh's Restaurant

Tirconnell Street; tel: 074-972 1262; www.oldecastlebar.com; food served daily noon–9pm; €€

An old stone-built bar across the street from the town's famous castle serves great bar food at lunch, including Irish stew (lamb and root vegetables in broth). At night the upstairs restaurant has a great reputation for local seafood, from battered haddock to oysters and lobster.

Northern Ireland: Belfast

Buskers

44 University Road; tel: 028-9020 2290; www.buskers.moondanceni.co.uk; Tue–Thu noon–9pm, Fri–Sat until 10pm, Sun until 8.30pm; ££

Located in the heart of Queen's Quarter on a Victorian terrace that has retained its original character. Music is an important focus for this restaurant, with the soundtrack carefully selected to create the perfect backdrop to home-made food that speaks for itself.

Coco

7–11 Linenhall Street; tel: 028-9031 1150; www.cocobelfast.com; Mon–Fri noon–3pm, Mon–Sat 5pm–late, Sun 1–9pm; ££

Opened in 2009, Coco quickly gained a reputation as one of the best and cool-

Mourne Seafood Bar, Belfast

est restaurants in the city. Owned by a talented local chef Jason More, the eclectic interior is complemented by a no-nonsense menu.

Deane's Deli + Bistro

44 Bedford Street; tel: 028-9024 8800; www.michaeldeane.ie; Mon–Sat noon–3pm, 5.30–10pm; ££

Deane's Deli is part of the restaurant empire of innovative Belfast chef Michael Deane. A relaxed café during the day, with fabulous cheese, meat and antipasti boards, it turns into an atmospheric 'vin-café' by night. The delicious food is locally sourced and cooked with a delicate touch. The fish specials – local hake with chorizo, or whole baked monkfish – are a must.

Ginger

6–8 Hope Street; tel: 028-9024 4421; www.gingerbistro.com; Thu–Sat noon–3pm, Mon 5–9pm, Tue–Thu until 9.30pm, Fri–Sat until 10pm; £££

Young owner-chef Simon McCance cooks in a contemporary style, aiming to keep the food as fresh and simple as possible. In spite of its central location near the famous Crown Liquor Saloon, Ginger has the buzz and friendliness of a neighbourhood restaurant.

James Street South

21 James Street South; tel: 028-9043 4310; www.jamesstreetsouth.co.uk; Mon–Sat 5.30pm–late, also Wed–Sat 12.30–2.30pm; £££

An exceptional place. Exciting, innovative, top-class cooking with service to match. Classic French menu.

Metro Kitchen

Crescent Townhouse Hotel, 13 Lower Crescent; tel: 028-9032 3349; www.crescenttownhouse.com; daily 5.30–9.30pm; £££

This elegant brasserie just off Botanic Avenue offers modern Irish and British cooking with a twist; try the slow-roast pork ribs, Glenarm salmon or beef and stout pie. There's also a good vegetarian menu and an excellent choice of wines.

Mourne Seafood Bar

34–36 Bank Street; tel: 028-9024 8544; www.mourneseafood.com; Mon–Thu noon–9.30pm, Fri–Sat noon–4pm, 5–10pm, Sun 1–6pm; ££

One of the city's favourite restaurants, this seafood bar serves up the daily catch from the owners' beds in Carlingford Lough, and the ports of Annalong and Kilkeel in County Down. The Mourne seafood casserole is renowned.

Neill's Hill Brasserie

229 Upper Newtownards Road; tel: 028-9065 0079; www.neillshill.com; Mon–Thu 10am–9.30pm, Fri–Sat until 10pm, Sun until 8pm; ££

Modern restaurant serving great wholesome favourites. Extensive menu of seafood and local meat, with daily specials on the blackboard, and consistently good cooking and service.

NIGHTLIFE

Aside from Irish dancing and Irish pubs, Ireland offers state-of-the-art theatres and concert venues. Some of the main venues are listed here.

The Irish will gladly pursue the *craic* for several hours until they find it. The two capitals and Cork, Galway, Limerick and Sligo all have thriving live music scenes; check the local papers for details or ask around, particularly in smaller towns. A local barperson will usually know which bar or venue has live sounds that evening. Impromptu music sessions, or even recitations of stories or poetry, are common.

In Dublin, the Button Factory (Curved Street; http://buttonfactory.ie/) hosts an eclectic line-up of hip-hop, electro, dance and indie; for comedy, rock and folk, head to Vicar St (58–59 Thomas Street; www.vicarstreet.com). Dublin's longest-running and best-loved rock venues is Whelans (25 Wexford Street; www. whelanslive.com). In Belfast, try The John Hewitt (51 Donegall Street; www.thejohn hewitt.com) for blues, jazz and folk, or Madden's Bar (74 Berry Street) for traditional Irish music.

Dublin

Abbey Theatre
Lower Abbey Street; tel: 01-878 7222; www.abbeytheatre.ie
Founded in 1903 by W.B. Yeats and Lady Gregory, the Abbey rejuvenated Irish literature and culture. Ireland's national theatre still features many Irish classics in its programme. The Abbey's sister theatre, the Peacock, stages new work.

Gaiety Theatre
South King Street; tel: 0818 719388; www.gaietytheatre.ie
A fine Victorian building, recently restored, with a programme that includes opera, ballet, pantomime, musicals and serious drama.

Gate Theatre
1 Cavendish Row, Parnell Square; tel: 01-874 4045; www.gatetheatre.ie
Founded in 1928, the Gate stages the classics of European, Irish and American theatre by playwrights such as Samuel Beckett, Brian Friel and Arthur Miller.

Olympia Theatre
72 Dame Street; tel: 01-679 3323; www.olympia.ie
One of the oldest theatres in Dublin, the Olympia was once a Victorian music hall; now it is used both as a theatre and as a venue for live bands.

Project Arts Centre
39 East Essex Street, Temple Bar; tel: 01-881 9613; www.projectartscentre.ie
Stages cutting-edge theatre, dance and music, as well as contemporary art exhibitions.

Abbey Theatre, Dublin

Samuel Beckett Theatre

Trinity College; tel: 01-896 1334;
www.tcd.ie/beckett-theatre

The Beckett is based in the university that produced such dramatists as Goldsmith, Synge and Beckett himself, and is run in association with the university's Samuel Beckett Centre. It's a venue for both the Dublin Fringe and Dublin Theatre festivals.

Southwest: Cork city

Cork Opera House

Emmet Place; tel: 021-427 0022;
www.corkoperahouse.ie

Cork's principal theatre since the late 19th century offers drama, musicals, family shows, dance and comedy.

Everyman Palace

15 MacCurtain Street; tel: 021-450 1673;
www.everymancork.com

This 650-seat late-Victorian theatre stages drama and musicals, and also hosts club nights.

Southwest: Tralee

Siamsa Tíre: National Folk Theatre of Ireland

Town Park, Tralee; tel: 066-712 3055;
www.siamsatire.com

The Irish rural tradition is celebrated here in song, dance and mime.

West: Limerick city

Lime Tree Theatre

Mary Immaculate College, Courtbrack Avenue; tel: 061-953 400; www.limetreetheatre.ie

A modern, 510-seat theatre that stages music, comedy, drama and traditional arts.

West: Ennis

Glór Irish Music Centre

Causeway Link; tel: 065-684 3103;
www.glor.ie

A modern building with two auditoria. Irish music shows in summer; theatre and comedy for the rest of the year.

West: Galway city

Druid Theatre Company

Druid Lane Theatre, Druid Lane; tel: 091-568 660; www.druidtheatre.com

One of Ireland's most successful repertory theatre companies presents a mix of new work and revivals in its refurbished 90-seat theatre. Other companies perform at the 400-seat Town Hall Theatre (Courthouse Square; 091-569777; www.tht.ie).

Northwest: Sligo town

Hawk's Well Theatre

Temple Street; tel: 071-916 1518;
www.hawkswell.com

A modern theatre that hosts touring and local shows; home of the annual W.B. Yeats International Summer School.

Northern Ireland: Belfast

Grand Opera House

Great Victoria Street; tel: 028-9024 1919;
www.goh.co.uk

This glorious 1895 building is Belfast's biggest entertainment venue, staging drama, musicals, ballet and pantomime.

Grand Opera House, Belfast

Lyric Theatre

Ridgeway Street; tel: 028-9038 1081; www.lyrictheatre.co.uk
Northern Ireland's only full-time producing theatre has an £18m state-of-the-art building on the banks of the River Lagan with a bar and café.

The MAC

Hurst House, 18–19 Corporation Square; tel: 028-9023 5053; www.themaclive.com
A multi-discipline arts centre in Belfast's Cathedral Quarter with two theatres and three art galleries.

Waterfront Hall

2 Lanyon Place; tel: 028-9033 4400; www.waterfront.co.uk
A multi-purpose venue offering comedy, theatre, music and conferences, with two exhibition galleries.

Nightclubs

Dublin
Button Factory

Curved Street, Temple Bar, Dublin 2, tel: 01-670 9105, www.buttonfactory.ie
Probably Dublin's best-known venue for exciting live music, from rock to dance and electro, frequented by music buffs as well as clubbers.

La Cave

28 South Anne Street, Dublin 2, tel: 01-679 4409, www.lacavewinebar.com
Tiny, late-night venue which falls somewhere between a restaurant, wine bar and nightclub, although there's no dance floor as such. The Latino sounds and intimate atmosphere make this a favourite with an eclectic crowd wanting to kick back well into the wee small hours.

Copper Face Jacks

29-30 Harcourt Street, Dublin 2, tel: 01-425 5300, http://copperfacejacks.ie
For when you don't feel like posing and just want to bop the night away to chart, dance and R&B.

Farrier & Draper

Powerscourt Townhouse Centre, South William St, Dublin 2, tel: 01-677 1220, www.farrieranddraper.ie
Cool late-night destination for a style-conscious crowd to lounge in Georgian splendour. Amazing interiors in bars spread over three levels with an Italian restaurant in the basement.

The George

89 South Great George's Street, Dublin 2, tel: 01-478 2983, www.thegeorge.ie
Probably the city's most popular gay club. The George pub from which the club gets its name is a favourite meeting place among gay men. Stylish dress.

House

27 Lower Leeson Street, Dublin 2, tel: 01-905 9090, www.housedublin.ie
Ultra-hip venue where everyone who's anyone in rock music, the media and modelling congregate. The dance floor is home to the young and beautiful.

Lillie's Bordello

Adam Court, Grafton Street, Dublin 2, tel: 01-679 9204, www.lilliesbordello.ie

One of the most exclusive clubs in town, and one that prides itself on its VIP lounge where high-profile party animals rub shoulders with fellow celebrities. Non-members are not guaranteed entry.

Octagon Bar at the Clarence Hotel

6–8 Wellington Quay, Dublin 2, tel: 01-407 0800 (hotel reception), www.theclarence.ie

This octagon-shaped, honey-coloured bar is the place to see and be seen in Dublin. The cocktails (€8–15) are world-class and excellent value. Try the flavoured daiquiris or the delicious 'Bramble' (a gin-based cocktail).

Sin

17-19 Sycamore St, Dublin 2, tel: 01-633 4700, www.sinbar.ie

Sin proudly bills itself as Dublin's number one club for house music with top Irish and international DJs spinning the decks every weekend.

Sugar Club

8 Lower Leeson Street, Dublin 2, tel: 01-678 7188, www.thesugarclub.com

Live bands most nights are followed by DJ sets. The bar has one of the city's most extensive cocktail menus.

Vicar Street

58–59 Thomas Street, Dublin 8, tel: 01-775 5800, www.vicarstreet.ie

A hugely successful music venue opposite Christchurch Cathedral, with seats for 1,050, or 1,500 standing.

The Workman's Club

10 Wellington Quay, Dublin 2, tel: 01-670 6692, http://theworkmansclub.com/

This live music venue is spread over two floors and has played host to some legendary acts over the years. Right in the centre of Temple Bar.

Belfast

Limelight

17 Ormeau Avenue, tel: 028-9032 7007, www.limelightbelfast.com

One of Belfast's longest established and best venues for live music and club nights.

Northern Whig

2 Bridge Street, tel: 028-9050 9888, www.thenorthernwhig.com

Housed in what was once an old Belfast newspaper office. Don't miss the three granite statues of socialist workers rescued from Soviet-era Prague after the fall of communism. It gets heaving on weekends.

Robinson's

38–40 Great Victoria Street, tel: 028-9024 7447

This complex, next to the Crown, includes the now rather dated-looking but still popular Irish-themed pub, Fibber Magee's, but also the quirkily upmarket BT1, and Roxy, home to dance nights and live music.

Playing by St Patrick's in Dublin

A–Z

A

Age restrictions

The age of consent is 17. At 17 you can apply for a driver's licence. The legal drinking age is 18, but some pubs will only serve those over 21 carrying photo ID. You must be 18 to buy cigarettes and tobacco. In the Republic of Ireland under 18s are not allowed on premises that serve alcohol after 9.30pm.

B

Budgeting

The cost of a pint of draught beer in the Republic starts from €3.80; wine from about €4.50 for 175ml. Beer costs approximately €5–€6 a pint in Dublin, and wine about €5.50 a glass, but it could be more in a fashionable bar and up to twice as much in a five-star hotel.

A main course at a budget restaurant costs €10–€15, at a moderate one €18–28 and at an expensive one €28–35.

A double room with breakfast costs about €70–€100 at a B&B or guesthouse, €100–€180 at a moderate hotel and €180–€220 at an expensive hotel.

Restaurant and hotel prices in Northern Ireland are roughly comparable, although groceries and other products are often cheaper in Northern Ireland than in the Republic.

A taxi from Dublin airport to the city centre costs about €25. A single bus ticket in Dublin or Cork costs €2.70, and a Dublin tram (Luas) ticket costs €2.40 for a similar distance. A one-day Combi ticket for both bus and tram in Dublin costs €11.70.

Admission to national museums in both the Republic and Northern Ireland is free. Charges for other heritage attractions vary from €3–€12 and up. A Heritage Card (adult: €49, family: €90) gives free admission to over 90 national sights and monuments (www.heritageireland.ie). From Dublin Tourism, you can buy a pass that gives free admission to 25 sights plus other concessions (for one day, adult: €49, child: €29; www.dublinpass.com).

C

Children

Irish people love children. They are usually welcome at hotels and B&Bs, most of which can supply special cots or babysitting services. Many hotels allow children to stay in their parents' room at no extra charge; check when booking. Some of the grander country houses will only accept children over 12.

Most restaurants can supply highchairs and a children's menu. Kids are

Ha'Penny Bridge, Dublin   *Looking out over the Cliffs of Moher*

generally welcome in pubs up to about 7pm (and by law under 18s must be gone by 9.30pm), but this is at the discretion of the landlord.

During holiday periods, there are plenty of child-oriented activities organised by museums, local festivals and outdoor centres; tourist offices will have full details.

Clothing

You can safely leave your formal clothes at home, unless you are going to the Wexford Festival Opera. Smart-casual is acceptable just about everywhere. Because of the unpredictability of the weather, pack an umbrella, some rainproof clothing and a warm sweater, even in summer. But bring sun cream as well; it does shine sometimes.

Crime and safety

While rural Ireland is a low-risk area for crime, hired cars are easy targets for criminals, and thefts from cars are commonplace in Dublin, other major towns and cities, and in the car parks of visitor attractions. Never leave anything visible in your car, even if you are only leaving it briefly. Be careful when withdrawing money from ATMs, and shield your pin number. Beware of pickpockets in crowded places. In central Dublin ask your hotel whether it is safe to walk home in the dark (take particular care around the Lower Gardiner Street and Connolly Station).

It is sensible to keep a copy of your passport in case of theft.

Victims of crime in the Republic should contact Irish Tourist Assistance Service, Pearse Garda Station, Dublin 2; tel: 1890-365 700; www.itas.ie.

Customs

Visitors of all nationalities entering or leaving the EU via Ireland or Northern Ireland must declare on arrival or departure sums of cash above €10,000.

Visitors within the EU may import the following goods, provided they were purchased within the EU and are for personal use: 800 cigarettes, 400 cigarillos, 200 cigars, 1kg tobacco, 10 litres spirits, 20 litres fortified wines, 90 litres wine, 110 litres beer.

From outside the EU you may import duty-free: 200 cigarettes or the tobacco equivalent, 4 litres of wine or 1 litre of spirits, and other goods to the value of €430 per person.

For details of restricted goods, see www.revenue.ie.

Non-EU visitors can claim back sales taxes on purchases made in the Republic. Participating stores have a 'Tax Free Shopping' sign in the window. If the item is priced at €2000 or more, you must present the tax refund documentation and the goods to customs on departure. Some airports will refund you on the spot; otherwise, mail the validated document back to the store and a refund will be issued. The VAT rate on most items is 23 percent.

D

Disabled travellers

Ireland is still introducing facilities such as ramps and accessible toilets for people with disabilities. Public transport in Dublin is now excellent but some parts of the country lag behind. However, visitors with disabilities often find that people's helpfulness makes up for the lack of amenities.

In the Republic, the key organisation for practical information, wheelchair rental and parking permits is the Irish Wheelchair Association (Áras Chúchulainn, Blackheath Drive, Clontarf, Dublin; tel: 01-818 6400; www.iwa.ie). The official government body is the National Disability Authority (25 Clyde Road, Ballsbridge, Dublin 4; tel: 01-608 0400; www.nda.ie). The Head Office of Fáilte Ireland (88-95 Amiens St, Dublin 1; tel: 1800 242 473; www.failteireland.com) can advise on attractions and accommodation suitable for disabled visitors.

In Northern Ireland, Disability Action (Portside Business Park, 189 Airport Road West, Belfast; tel: 028-9029 7880; www.disabilityaction.org) offers practical advice.

E

Electricity

220 volts AC (50 cycles) is standard. Hotels usually have dual 220/110 voltage sockets for electric razors only. Most sockets require a 3-pin plug; visitors may need an adaptor.

Embassies and consulates

Dublin

Australia. Fitzwilton House, Wilton Terrace, Dublin 2; tel: 01-664 5300; www.ireland.embassy.gov.au.

Britain. 29 Merrion Road, Dublin 4; tel: 01-205 3700; www.britishembassyinireland.fco.gov.uk.

Canada. 7–8 Wilton Terrace, Dublin 2; tel: 01-234 4000; www.canada.ie.

US. 42 Elgin Road, Dublin 4; tel: 01-668 8777; https://ie.usembassy.gov.

Belfast

American Consulate General. Danesfort House, 223 Stranmillis Road, Belfast BT9 5GR; tel: 028-9038 6100; http://belfast.usconsulate.gov.

Emergencies

In an emergency, dial 999; 112 is also used in the Republic.

Etiquette

The Irish love to talk, and they expect visitors to respond in kind. Strike up a conversation with the person sitting next to you at the bar or on the bus, and be prepared to tell your life story. Pub etiquette is based on good manners: if somebody buys you a drink, buy one back. Avoid being drawn into discussions of politics or religion while alcohol is being consumed. Avoid telling people what's wrong with their country (eg the

Slieve League cliffs in County Donegal

roads, the signposts, the high cost of everything); they know already.

G

Gay and lesbian travellers

There should be no major problems for gay and lesbian travellers in Ireland. Be as safety conscious as you would in any foreign city or country. Openly gay couples may attract unwanted attention in small-town pubs.

Information on LGBT-friendly bars and clubs, accommodation, advice and contacts can be found through the following organisations:

Dublin. Outhouse, 51 Capel Street; tel: 01-873 4999; www.outhouse.ie; and Gay Switchboard, tel: 01-872 1055; www.gayswitchboard.ie.

Cork. Cork Gay Project, 4 South Terrace; tel: 021-430 0430; www.gayproject cork.com.

West of the Shannon. Out West Ireland, PO Box 58, Castlebar, County Mayo; tel: 094-937 3479; www.out west.ie.

Belfast. Queer Space, 3rd Floor, Belfast LGBT Centre, 28–31 Waring Street, BT1 2DX; www.queerspace.org.uk.

Green issues

Ireland has an active Green Party, but green issues and sustainable planning are minority concerns. Recycling is in its infancy, and much waste still goes to landfill; however, a small charge for plastic bags in supermarkets has been effective. Solar energy and wind power are also nascent, although there are controversial plans for giant wind farms in the west. Many of Ireland's smaller farms are now managed under REPs (Rural Environment Protection Scheme), to encourage wildlife and biological diversity. But overuse of fertilizer in farming and forestry has led to pollution of lakes and rivers.

For the latest, visit www.friendsoftheirishenvironment.org.

H

Health

Medical insurance is advisable for all visitors. However, visitors from EU countries are entitled to medical treatment in the Republic and Northern Ireland under reciprocal arrangements.

With the exception of UK citizens, visitors from EU states should obtain the European Health Insurance Card, which entitles the holder to treatment through the public health system if you get ill on a temporary stay in Ireland. If hospital treatment is necessary, this will be given free on a public ward. UK visitors need only go to a doctor (or, in an emergency, a hospital), present some proof of identity (eg a driving licence) and request treatment under the EU health agreement.

Hospitals and pharmacies

Dublin. St Vincent's University Hospital, Merrion Road, Dublin 4; tel: 01-221 4000; www.stvincents.ie.

Dublin bus tours

Hickey's Pharmacy, 55 Lower O'Connell Street; tel: 01-873 0427; www.hickeyspharmacies.ie. Also branches on Grafton St and Henry St.

McCabe's Late Night Pharmacy, Dundrum Town Centre; tel: 01-298 6709; www.mccabespharmacy.com. Open until 11pm 7 nights a week

Belfast. Belfast City Hospital, 51 Lisburn Road; tel: 028-9032 9241.

Urban Pharmacy, 56 Dublin Road, BT2 7HN; tel: 028-9024 6336.

Hours and holidays

Shops and department stores usually open Mon–Sat 9.30am–6 or 7pm and Sun noon–6pm. In smaller towns some shops close for lunch between 1pm and 2pm. Supermarkets and convenience stores generally open daily until 9pm. Post offices open Mon–Fri 9am–5.30pm and Sat 9am–1pm. Government offices are open Mon–Fri 9am–5pm.

Museums and other tourist sights are often closed on Monday, and outside Dublin and Belfast most have restricted opening hours between November and Easter or late May.

In hotels and B&Bs, breakfast is generally served from 8–10am, and in restaurants and pubs until noon. Restaurants and pubs generally serve lunch between 12.30 and 2.30pm, and dinner from 6 to 9.30pm.

Public holidays
1 Jan: New Year's Day
17 Mar: St Patrick's Day
Mar/Apr: Good Fri and Easter Mon
1st Mon May: Early May Bank Holiday
Last Mon May: Bank Holiday (NI)
1st Mon June: Bank Holiday (RoI)
12 July: Bank Holiday (NI)
1st Mon Aug: Bank Holiday (RoI)
Last Mon Aug: Bank Holiday (NI)
Last Mon Oct: Bank Holiday (RoI)
25 Dec: Christmas Day
26 Dec: St Stephen's Day (RoI) Boxing Day (NI)

I

Internet facilities

Wi-fi is widely available free in cafés, bars and public areas of hotels.

M

Maps

Cyclists and walkers may want small-scale maps; these can be bought locally from bookshops, newsagents and tourist offices. The latter usually also offer a free town and surrounding area map.

Media

Print media. *The Irish Times* is Ireland's newspaper of record, with good coverage of foreign news, arts and business. The *Irish Independent* is published daily in Dublin, and the *Irish Examiner* in Cork. Two morning papers are published in Belfast, the *Belfast Newsletter* and *Irish News*. Each city also publishes an evening paper, useful for entertainment listings.

Letter box with the modern Irish Gaelic name for Dublin

Television and radio. In the Republic RTÉ (www.rte.ie) broadcasts three channels including Irish-language TG4 (www.tg4.ie). Most UK channels are available on satellite or cable TV, which is widespread in hotels and B&Bs (confirm on booking). In Northern Ireland, the BBC Northern Ireland (www.bbc.com/northernireland) includes local coverage.

In the Republic, RTÉ1 is the main radio station for news, current affairs and drama, 2FM plays pop music and Lyric FM is for lovers of classical music. National commercial radio stations Newstalk and Today FM are very popular. There are also a number of independent local radio stations, such as Shannonside FM in the midwest. In Northern Ireland the commercial-free BBC Radio Ulster has full local coverage, as do Downtown Radio and Cool FM.

Money

Currency. The Republic of Ireland is in the Eurozone. Banknotes come in denominations of €5, €10, €20, €50, €100, €200 and €500, coins in denominations of 10, 20 and 50 cents, €1 and €2. In Northern Ireland, the British pound (£) is the standard currency, although most traders in border areas are prepared to accept euros. Banknotes: £5, £10, £20 and £50; coins: 1p, 2p, 5p, 10p, 20p, 50p, £1 and £2.

Banking hours. Banks are open Mon–Fri 10am–4pm, with one day late opening until 5pm (Thu in Dublin). AIB on Grafton St is open Mon–Fri 8am–7pm (Thu until 9pm) and Sat–Sun 10am–6pm. Smaller town banks may close for lunch from 12.30–1.30pm.

Cash machines. Nearly all banks have 24-hour cash machines (ATMs), but not all towns have banks. In smaller places, cash machines can be found in convenience stores. Check with your bank before leaving home to confirm that your bankcard will work in Ireland.

Credit cards. The most widely accepted cards are Visa and Mastercard, followed by American Express. Many but not all guest houses and B&Bs take credit cards; check in advance.

Tipping. Tipping is not expected in bars, except in lounge bars where drinks are brought to your table. It is usual to give at least a 10 percent tip to waiting staff. Round taxi fares to the nearest euro or pound, and porters are given about €1 or £1 a bag.

P

Police

The Republic is policed by the Garda Síochána (Guardians of the Peace), and Northern Ireland by the Police Service of Northern Ireland (PSNI). In an emergency, dial 999; 112 is also used in the Republic.

Post

Postage stamps are sold by post offices, newsagents and general stores. Letters and postcards cost 72 cents to send

Cycling in Wicklow

within the Republic and €1.10 to the UK, mainland Europe and North America; they cost 64p within the UK, £1.05 to Europe and the rest of the world. In the Republic most letterboxes are pillar-shaped and are painted green; in Northern Ireland the letterboxes are red. Note that Republic of Ireland stamps may not be used on mail posted in Northern Ireland and vice versa.

Post offices. Hours are generally Mon–Fri 9am–5.30pm and Sat 9am–1pm. The General Post Offices in the two capitals are at O'Connell Street, Dublin (tel: 01-705 7000) and 12/16 Bridge Street, Belfast (tel: 0845-611 2970).

S

Smoking

Smoking is banned in all workplaces, including taxis, bars, restaurants and nightclubs. Elaborate sheltered outdoor smoking areas are provided by many pubs and clubs.

T

Telephones

The international dialling code for the Republic of Ireland is 353. Northern Ireland's is 44. If you are calling the North from the Republic, just substitute the code 028 with 048, rather than using the international dialling code.

There are several telecommunications companies operating in Ireland, the largest one being Eir (www.eir.ie).

Public telephones mainly use phone cards, which are widely available from newsagents and supermarkets. Phone boxes are gradually disappearing, as the mobile phone gains dominance. International calls can be dialled direct from private phones, or dial 1901 for customer service. For directory enquiries dial 11811, for international directory enquiries 11818. The long-distance services of BT Ireland, AT&T, Sprint and MCI are also available.

Services in Northern Ireland are operated by British Telecom (www.bt.com); dial 100 for the operator.

Mobile (cell) phones. Only mobiles with GSM will work in Ireland. If your phone is non-GSM, consult with your provider before travelling. It may be cheaper to buy a local SIM card and top up with prepaid calls. Local providers include 3, Meteor, Tesco Mobile and Virgin Mobile Ireland. If you are coming from the UK, your mobile should work in Northern Ireland, but you will need international roaming in the Republic.

Time zones

Ireland follows Greenwich Mean Time. In spring, the clock moves one hour ahead for Summer Time; in autumn it moves back to GMT. At noon – according to GMT – it is 4am in Los Angeles, 7am in New York, 1pm in western Europe, 8pm in Singapore, 10pm in Sydney and midnight in New Zealand.

Walking to the beach at Lahinch, County Clare

Tourist information

Fáilte Ireland Dublin Head Office. 88–95 Amiens Street; tel: 1800 242 473; www.discoverireland.ie. (For tourist information, tel: 0800 313 4000 in the UK.)

Dublin Tourism Centre. Suffolk Street (near Grafton Street); tel: 01-605 7700; www.visitdublin.com.

Regional offices. Local tourist offices can be found throughout Ireland. A number are mentioned in the tours in this guide; otherwise, for details see www.discoverireland.ie.

Northern Ireland Tourist Board. 59 North Street, Belfast BT1 1NB; tel: 028-9023 1221; www.discovernorthernireland.com.

Transport

Arrival by air

There are flights from Britain and Europe to Belfast, Dublin, Cork and Shannon airports, with more than 30 airlines flying from over 70 destinations. There are also frequent flights from British airports to regional airports in Kerry, Galway, Waterford and Knock (County Mayo).

The main carriers from Britain are Aer Lingus (www.aerlingus.com), British Airways (www.britishairways.com), easyJet (www.easyjet.com) and Ryanair (www.ryanair.com).

There are direct flights from the US to both Dublin and Shannon airports and Belfast International Airport. The main carriers are Aer Lingus (www.aerlingus.com), American Airlines (www.aa.com), United (www.united.com), Delta Airlines (www.delta.com) and US Airways (www.usairways.com).

Airport to city

Republic. There is a regular bus service from **Dublin Airport** (tel: 01-814 1111; www.dublinairport.com) to the main bus station in the city centre (30 min), while Aircoach (www.aircoach.ie) departs every 10–20 minutes for various city locations. The bus from **Cork Airport** (tel: 021-431 3131; www.corkairport.com) to the city takes about 10 minutes. From **Shannon Airport** (tel: 061-712 000; www.shannonairport.com) there is a regular bus service to Limerick city (30 min) and other main cities.

A **taxi** from the airport to the city centre should cost approximately €25 in Dublin, €12 in Cork and €35 in Shannon (to Limerick).

Northern Ireland. There are two major airports: **Belfast International**, (tel: 028-9448 4848; www.belfastairport.com) a 30-minute bus ride from town or about £30 by taxi, and **George Best Airport** (tel: 028-9093 9093; www.belfastcityairport.com), a short bus or taxi ride from the town centre. For more information on access to and from airports see www.discoverireland.com.

Arrival by sea

Ireland has five main ferry ports; Republic: Cork, Dublin, and Rosslare (County Wexford); Northern Ireland: Belfast and

Larne (County Antrim). For details of operators and routes, see www.discover ireland.com.

Public transport in Ireland

Outside Dublin in the Republic, public transport can be limited. **Bus Éireann** (01-836 6111; www.buseireann. ie) serves provincial Ireland with both local and direct express services. Its Expressway timetable (available online) is essential if you plan to travel by bus, and its Open Road passes allow flexible cross-country travel. Dublin's main bus station (Busáras) is on Store Street.

Iarnród Éireann (Irish Rail; 01-836 6222; www.irishrail.ie) runs rail services from Connolly, Pearse Street and Heuston stations to the main towns in Ireland, including Belfast. Fares are reasonable (eg Dublin–Cork return: €51, Dublin–Galway return: €33). Irish Rail also has a limited number of cut-price tickets available online.

The Republic is one of 21 countries in which you can use the global Eurailpass (www.eurail.com).

For details on public transport by bus and rail in Northern Ireland (and the Metro bus company in Belfast), call 028-9066 6630 or visit www.translink. co.uk.

Public transport in Dublin

Dublin Bus (tel: 01-873 4222; www. dublinbus.ie) has an extensive network within the greater Dublin area, with priority bus lanes ensuring progress through the often gridlocked traffic. Dublin Bus requires exact change to be given, and will not accept notes.

The bus network is supplemented by the **Luas** tram system (tel: 1850 300604 within Republic; www.luas.ie). Purchase of a one, seven or thirty day Flexi ticket allows for unlimited travel on the Luas. Leap cards are valid for Dublin Bus and the Luas, widely available from newsagents, and will give the best value. For ticket costs, see Budgeting.

The **DART** (www.irishrail.ie), a rapid transit railway, runs from the city centre along the coast from Howth in the north to Greystones in the south.

Taxis

There are metered taxis in Belfast, Cork, Dublin, Galway and Limerick. In other areas, fares should be agreed beforehand. Taxis are usually found at ranks in central locations, or booked by phone, and do not usually cruise the streets. **NRC Taxis** (tel. 01-677 2222; www.nrc.ie) is one of the biggest Dublin companies.

Driving

Outside the cities, Irish roads are still among the least congested in Europe, although it is hard to believe this when you are stuck in a traffic jam in Dublin's ever-expanding suburbs.

Rules of the road. Drive on the left on both sides of the border. All passengers must wear seat belts. Drink driving laws are strict, and it is an offence to drive

Dublin cabs

with a concentration of alcohol exceeding 50mg per 100ml of blood.

Remember that in the Republic speed limit signs are in kilometres. The limit is 50km/h (31mph) in urban areas, 80km/h (50mph) on non-national roads, 100km/h (62mph) on national routes (green signposts) and 120km/h (75mph) on motorways. On-the-spot fines can be issued for speeding offences.

In Northern Ireland, the limit in urban areas is 30mph (48km/h), on country roads 60mph (96km/h), and 70mph (113km/h) on motorways and dual-carriageway trunk roads.

Tolls. There are toll charges for using the M50 Dublin orbital motorway, M3 south and north bound and the M1 northern motorway, the Dublin Port tunnel, Limerick tunnel, the Waterford bypass and some sections of rural motorway. Visit www.eflow.ie for information on barrier-free tolling.

Car hire. Be sure to book in advance for July and August. Car hire is expensive in Ireland, and advance booking as part of a fly-drive or train-ferry-drive package often leads to a better deal, as does booking online. Drivers under 25 and over 70 may have to pay a higher rate. Most companies will not rent cars to people over 76. If you intend to drive across the border, inform your rental company beforehand to check that you are fully insured.

Local and international car hire companies in both the Republic and Northern Ireland are listed on www.irelandcarhire.com.

V

Visas and passports

UK citizens do not require a passport to enter Ireland, but most carriers by air or sea ask for photographic ID, usually either a passport or driving licence. Check with the individual company before travelling.

Non-UK nationals must have a valid passport. EU nationals and travellers from the US, Canada, Australia, New Zealand and South Africa are simply required to show a passport. Visitors of all other nationalities should contact their local Irish embassy or consulate before travelling to the Republic, or their British Embassy, High Commission or Consular Office before travelling to Northern Ireland.

W

Websites

www.ireland.com and www.discoverireland.ie – the official tourism websites of Failte Ireland
www.discovernorthernireland.com – detailed information on the North
www.entertainment.ie – for theatre, cinema, club and festival listings
www.bandbireland.com – accommodation reservation network of B&B Ireland
www.hostels-ireland.com – Tourist Board-approved holiday hostels
www.met.ie – for the latest forecast

BOOKS AND FILM

Books

Irish classics

Gulliver's Travels by Jonathan Swift (1667–1745). The Dean of Dublin's St Patrick's Cathedral was also a great satirist; this book is a savage indictment of mankind's folly.

The Vicar of Wakefield by Oliver Goldsmith (1728–74). A graduate of Trinity College, Dublin, like many others he headed for London where he achieved fame for his work.

Castle Rackrent by Maria Edgeworth. Published in 1800, Edgeworth's novel uses pointed humour to question Anglo-Irish identity and absentee landlords.

The Complete Works of Oscar Wilde (1854–1900). Besides his sparkling drawing room comedies, Wilde also wrote poetry, essays, charming children's stories and a novel.

The Complete Works of W.B. Yeats (1865–1939). Winner of the 1923 Nobel Prize for Literature, he was also a founder of the National Theatre and a Senator.

Dracula by Bram Stoker (1847–1912). The most famous novel of Dublin-born Stoker's large output.

The Playboy of the Western World by J.M. Synge (1871–1909). The masterpiece of a multi-faceted writer who invented a new language using the poetry inherent in the Irish vernacular. Its earthy realism caused riots at its Abbey premiere.

Portrait of the Artist as a Young Man; Dubliners; Ulysses by James Joyce (1882–1941). His coming-of-age novel and the collection of Dublin stories will help you decide whether to tackle his magnum opus, *Ulysses*.

Shadow of a Gunman; Juno and the Paycock; The Plough and the Stars by Sean O'Casey (1880–1964). His trilogy of tragicomedies is set in the Dublin tenements, and deals with the problems of ordinary families caught up in historic events.

Essential contemporary fiction and poetry fiction

More Pricks than Kicks by Samuel Beckett. People are often surprised at how funny the Nobel Laureate's first story collection is, with its cast of outrageous Dublin characters.

Murphy by Samuel Beckett. Aspiring authors may be encouraged to know that this comic first novel was rejected by 41 publishers.

The Third Policeman by Flann O'Brien. Straight-faced novel of absurdist humour.

An Old Woman's Reflections by Peig Sayers. Memoir written in Irish by a natural storyteller about life on the Great Blasket Island.

The Islandman by Tomás O Crohan. Vivid memoir of a Great Blasket Island farmer-fisherman, written originally in Irish.

The Ginger Man by J.P. Donleavy. Exuberant, often hilarious, account of post-war Dublin, as seen by a hard-living American.

Langrishe, Go Down by Aidan Higgins. The last great Irish 'big house' novel, chronicling its decline, championed by Samuel Beckett and Harold Pinter.

The Country Girls; A Fanatic Heart: Selected Stories, Saints and Sinners by Edna O'Brien. Her first novel is a witty picture of Dublin in the 1950s, the stories are darker and deeper.

Troubles by J.G. Farrell. Wry, atmospheric account of sitting out the Civil War in a crumbling hotel.

The Book of Evidence and **The Sea** by John Banville. A leading intellectual and novelist, his 1989 novel is the disturbing story of a Dublin murderer, while his 2005 Booker Prize-winner is a tender account of lost love.

The South by Colm Tóibín. Now an internationally known novelist and travel writer, his first novel about an Irishwoman's love affair with Spain remains one of his best.

Collected Short Stories by William Trevor. Set in both England and Ireland, among the plain people. Trevor is a master of the quiet epiphany.

Creatures of the Earth: New and Selected Stories by John McGahern. One of the most understated and highly rated chroniclers of rural Ireland.

There are Little Kingdoms; Dark Lies the Island by Kevin Barry. Barry uses anarchic comedy to skewer the absurdities of post-Celtic Tiger rural Ireland. A name to watch.

All Names Have Been Changed by Claire Kilroy. A wry look at 1980s Ireland and its literary culture by an up-and-coming young novelist.

Poetry

Penguin Book of Contemporary Irish Poetry edited by Peter Fallon and Derek Mahon. Well-balanced selection of today's poets.

Collected Poems by Louis MacNeice. A major 20th-century poet, born in Ulster and educated in England, where he lived.

Collected Poems and **Finders Keepers** by Seamus Heaney. Superbly crafted lyric poems, and a collection of his incisive literary essays and lectures.

Collected Poems by Derek Mahon. A major 20th-century poet in the metaphysical mode, his more sophisticated œuvre is considered by many to be superior to Heaney's.

Collected Poems by Michael Longley. At his best, his perceptive lyrics, often nature-inspired, can stand beside fellow Ulster poets, Heaney and Mahon.

A Snail in My Prime by Paul Durcan. Popular, readable poet, known for his humour and honesty.

History

Luck and the Irish: A Brief History of Change, 1970–2000; Modern Ireland 1600–1972 by Roy Foster. Readable academic Irish history with many new insights.

The Story of Ireland: In Search of a New National Memory by Neil Hegarty. Book of the 2012 RTE TV series in which journalist Fergal Keane takes a fresh look at Irish history.

Ireland – A History by Robert Kee. Readable illustrated history, good on disentangling the Troubles.

How the Irish Saved Civilization by Thomas Cahill. A humorous look at Irish achievements down the years, with a serious core.

The Great Hunger: Ireland 1845–1849 by Cecil Woodham Smith. The classic account of the Famine is a harrowing but compelling narrative.

Biography

James Joyce by Richard Ellman. One of the finest literary biographies.

W.B. Yeats, a Life by R.F. Foster. Definitive two-volume life of the poet by leading historian.

Damned to Fame: A Life of Samuel Beckett by James Knowlson. The official biography.

Michael Collins by Tim Pat Coogan. The life of the pro-Treaty politician on which Neil Jordan's 1996 film was based.

Memoirs and journalism

Angela's Ashes by Frank McCourt. Bestselling account of a miserable childhood in Limerick.

Are You Somebody by Nuala O'Faolain. The 200-page introduction to the late author's collected journalism is admirably candid about her problems with alcohol and relationships.

To School Through the Fields by Alice Taylor. A simple account of a rural childhood in the 1940s, which became an international bestseller.

Films

The Quiet Man (1952). Directed by John Ford and starring John Wayne and Maureen O'Hara, this whimsical Hollywood portrayal of Ireland – filmed in Cong, County Mayo – appealed to the huge Irish-American audience. The Irish, who were in reality facing hardship and chronic emigration, didn't object to such a portrayal: indeed, they built a tourist industry on it.

Darby O'Gill and the Little People (1959). A pre-007 Sean Connery sings and dances with Janet Munro and gangs of diminutive actors. No cliché is left unturned and Walt Disney ended up with a pot of gold.

The Dead (1987). Veteran Hollywood director John Huston, who came of Irish stock and had a home in Ireland, captured the country's streak of Chekovian melancholy in his last film, adapted from a classic short story by James Joyce.

The Crying Game (1992). Neil Jordan explores the Troubles in Northern Ire-

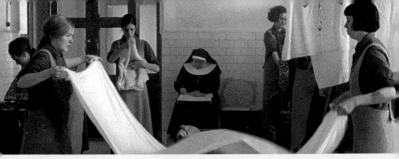

land and the conflict's impact on a complicated web of human relationships. An IRA member starts a romance with the girlfriend of a British soldier, leading to unexpected consequences.

Angela's Ashes (1999). Based on Frank McCourt's best-selling memoir (see opposite), Alan Parker's adaption slightly lacks the humour captured by McCourt. Some also felt it overstated the level of poverty, while others claimed the pain was driven out by glossy cinematography and sentimentality.

The Magdalene Sisters (2002). Peter Mullan's critically acclaimed film tells the story of the young girls – perhaps 30,000 of them over the years – who were sent to live-in convent laundries as a punishment for having premarital sex or becoming pregnant out of wedlock. These sadistic labour camps finally closed in the 1990s, and in 2012 Irish premier Enda Kenny officially apologised to the former residents.

Mickybo and Me (2004). Northern Irish comedy based on the stage play *Mojo Mickybo* by Owen McCafferty. Two young boys – one Catholic and one Protestant – become friends in the 1970s against the backdrop of the Troubles, sharing an obsession with *Butch Cassidy and the Sundance Kid*.

The Wind That Shakes the Barley (2006). The best recent film about the Irish Civil War, made by Englishman Ken Loach. It is set in 1920 and was filmed on location in rural Cork, starring Cillian Murphy.

Once (2007). This musical romance, funded by the Irish Film Board, explores the touching relationship between an Irish busker and a Czech musician, played by Glen Hansard and Markéta Irglová, who bond over music on the streets of Dublin. Won an Oscar for Best Song.

Garage (2007). Lenny Abrahamson (director) may have a name that sounds American but he is actually one of Ireland's success stories. The heart-wrenching *Garage* tells the story of a lonely garage attendant in a country town and won a prize at the Cannes Film Festival.

In Bruges (2008). The debut feature film of playwright Martin McDonagh, *In Bruges*, a black comedy starring Colin Farrell and Brendan Gleeson as a pair of Irish hitmen hiding out in Belgium's medieval city, proved an international triumph and raised the profile of the Irish film industry overseas.

Brooklyn (2015). Film based on Colm Tóibín's novel of the same name, about a young Irish girl who immigrates to Brooklyn from Enniscorthy in the 1950s.

Sing Street (2016). Coming-of-age comedy-drama written and directed by John Carney. Ferdia Walsh-Peelo plays Conor, a boy who finds escapism from his family home and his parents' relationship breakdown by forming a band in the hopes of impressing an older girl. Set against the backdrop of 1980s Dublin.

ABOUT THIS BOOK

This *Explore Guide* has been produced by the editors of Insight Guides, whose books have set the standard for visual travel guides since 1970. With top-quality photography and authoritative recommendations, these guidebooks bring you the very best routes and itineraries in the world's most exciting destinations.

BEST ROUTES

The routes in the book provide something to suit all budgets, tastes and trip lengths. As well as covering the destination's many classic attractions, the itineraries track lesser-known sights. The routes embrace a range of interests, so whether you are an art fan, a gourmet, a history buff or have kids to entertain, you will find an option to suit.

We recommend reading the whole of a route before setting out. This should help you to familiarise yourself with it and enable you to plan where to stop for refreshments – options are shown in the 'Food and Drink' box at the end of each tour.

For our pick of the tours by theme, consult Recommended Routes for… (see pages 6–7).

INTRODUCTION

The routes are set in context by this introductory section, giving an overview of the destination to set the scene, plus background information on food and drink, shopping and more, while a succinct history timeline highlights the key events over the centuries.

DIRECTORY

Also supporting the routes is a Directory chapter, with a clearly organised A–Z of practical information, our pick of where to stay while you are there and select restaurant listings; these eateries complement the more low-key cafés and restaurants that feature within the routes and are intended to offer a wider choice for evening dining. Also included here are some nightlife listings and our recommendations for books and films about the destination.

ABOUT THE AUTHORS

This new edition of *Explore Ireland* was updated by Mary Conneely, a Dublin-based travel writer. It builds on the edition written by Alannah Hopkin, who has lived in Kinsale since 1982, working as a writer and frequently contributing to Insight's Irish titles. The routes in Dublin, Belfast, and counties Wicklow, Sligo and Donegal were written by Tara Stubbs, who has a PhD in Irish literature and culture from Oxford University.

CONTACT THE EDITORS

We hope you find this Explore Guide useful, interesting and a pleasure to read. If you have any questions or feedback on the text, pictures or maps, please do let us know. If you have noticed any errors or outdated facts, or have suggestions for places to include on the routes, we would be delighted to hear from you. Please drop us an email at hello@insightguides.com. Thanks!

CREDITS

Explore Ireland
Editor: Helen Fanthorpe
Authors: Mary Conneely, Alannah Hopkin, Tara Stubbs, Jackie Staddon and Hilary Weston
Head of Production: Rebeka Davies
Update Production: Apa Digital
Picture Editor: Tom Smyth
Cartography: original cartography APA Cartography Department and Stephen Ramsay, updated by Carte
Photo credits: British Tourist Authority 97L; Corbis 27; Corrie Wingate/Apa Publications 4ML, 4MC, 4MR, 4MR, 4MC, 4ML, 6ML, 6BC, 7T, 7MR, 7M, 7MR, 8MC, 8ML, 8ML, 8MC, 8MR, 8MR, 12T, 13L, 13, 14, 15, 15L, 16, 17T, 17T, 17M, 19L, 20, 21L, 22, 23, 24, 25L, 26, 28MC, 28MR, 28ML, 28MR, 30, 31, 32, 33, 33L, 34, 35, 39L, 39, 40, 41, 41L, 42, 43L, 43, 44, 45, 45L, 70, 71L, 71, 72, 73, 73L, 75, 76, 77, 78, 79, 80, 81, 82, 83, 84, 85, 86, 87, 87L, 88, 89L, 89, 90, 91, 91L, 98ML, 98MC, 98MR, 98MR, 98MC, 98ML, 111, 124, 125, 125L, 126, 127, 128, 129, 130, 131, 133, 136; Dreamstime 46, 61, 67, 105, 110, 117; Fáilte Ireland 8/9, 48/49, 49L, 118, 134; Getty Images 4/5, 135; Glyn Genin/Apa Publications 6TL, 6MC, 25, 28ML, 37, 38, 47, 48, 50, 51, 53, 53L, 56, 58, 59, 60B, 60T, 63, 64T, 64B, 65, 65L, 68, 69; Granville Hotel 99T; iStock 18, 28MC, 57, 92, 93, 122; Kevin Cummins/Apa Publications 21, 54, 55, 94, 95, 95L, 123; Kobal 137; Leonardo 12B, 102, 103, 104, 106, 107, 109, 115, 116, 120/121; Northern Ireland Tourist Board 23L, 96/97, 119, 120; Tourism Ireland 1, 10/11, 18/19, 28/29, 52L, 96, 100/101, 112, 113
Cover credits: Shutterstock (main&bottom)

Printed by CTPS – China

Second Edition 2017

DISTRIBUTION

UK, Ireland and Europe
Apa Publications (UK) Ltd
sales@insightguides.com
United States and Canada
Ingram Publisher Services
ips@ingramcontent.com
Australia and New Zealand
Woodslane
info@woodslane.com.au
Southeast Asia
Apa Publications (Singapore) Pte
singaporeoffice@insightguides.com
Hong Kong, Taiwan and China
Apa Publications (HK) Ltd
hongkongoffice@insightguides.com
Worldwide
Apa Publications (UK) Ltd
sales@insightguides.com

SPECIAL SALES, CONTENT LICENSING AND COPUBLISHING

Insight Guides can be purchased in bulk quantities at discounted prices. We can create special editions, personalised jackets and corporate imprints tailored to your needs.
sales@insightguides.com
www.insightguides.biz

INDEX

MAP LEGEND

● Start of tour
→ Tour & route direction
❶ Recommended sight
❷ Recommended restaurant/café

★ Place of interest
ⓘ Tourist information
⚊ Statue/monument
✉ Main post office
🚌 Main bus station
— Four Courts LUAS tram line
– ∙ – National boundry
∙ – – – County boundry

▢ Park
▩ Important building
▤ Hotel
▤ Transport hub
▢ Shop / market
▢ Pedestrian area
▢ Urban area